Aussie STEM Stars

MICHELLE SIMMONS

Quantum computing scientist

Story told by NOVA WEETMAN

WILD DINGO PRESS

Aussie STEM Stars series
Published by Wild Dingo Press
Melbourne, Australia
books@wilddingopress.com.au
www.wilddingopress.com.au
www.aussieSTEMStars.com.au

This work was first published by Wild Dingo Press 2023

Cover Design: Gisela Beer
Illustrations: Mirjana Segan
Series Editor: Catherine Lewis
Printed in Australia
Weetman, Nova 1971–, author.
Michelle Simmons: Quantum computing scientist / Nova Weetman

A catalogue record for this book is available from the National Library of Australia

ISBN: 9781925893496 (paperback)
ISBN: 9781925893502 (ePDF)
ISBN: 9781925893519 (ePub)

Wild Dingo Press acknowledges the Traditional Owners of the country on which we work, the Wurundjeri people of the Kulin nation, and recognises their continuing connection to the land, waters and culture. We pay our respects to their Elders past and present.

Although my mother died soon after I reached adulthood,
and although she is not prominent in this story,
my mother had a very important influence.
Hardworking, kind and beautiful, Gloria Jean Simmons always
taught me to do my best and listen to my inner voice.

— Michelle Simmons

Disclaimer

This work has been developed in collaboration with Scientia Professor Michelle Simmons. The utmost care has been taken to respectfully portray, as accurately as memory allows, the events and the stories of all who appear in this work. The publisher assumes no liability or responsibility for unintended inaccuracies but would be pleased to rectify at the earliest opportunity any omissions or errors brought to their notice.

Contents

1
Odd one out

As usual, Michelle's dad and her older brother Gary were in the backyard playing football and as usual, they hadn't invited her to play. In fact, she'd been leaning up against the French windows for the last half hour and they hadn't even noticed she was there.

Whenever she asked if she could join in, one of them would always squirm out of it because they said she was only six and too young to play.

She bent down to tie up her shoelaces. She didn't have real football boots like Gary did with studs on the bottom so he could run fast on the grass. Hers were run-of-the-mill trainers with laces that worked their way free about 20 times a day.

'He lines up, he aims, he shoots...' Gary yelled, as he kicked the ball whizzing towards the glass windows and through the temporary goalposts that were just jumpers on the grass.

'And he scores!' Gary shouted, running in circles around their dad who was already returning the ball for the next pass.

Gary lived for football. He was an outstanding goalie who played for his local club. Each weekend after reading the weekly football fixtures he'd move on to the back of the newspaper, scanning the pages for results of his precious team, Arsenal. He had a red and white Arsenal towel, and an Arsenal scarf that he wore most days, even in summer.

If their dad wasn't around to kick the ball with him, then Gary would kick it around the garden over and over until their mum came out to tell him that it was time for dinner. Most weekends he was at the local park playing football with other boys from his team.

Michelle wasn't much interested in watching the game, even though it was nearly always on the TV at the weekends. She just wanted to play. To run around, steal the ball from Gary and his fast-moving feet, and maybe score a goal or two. Actually, it wouldn't have mattered if it was football, gardening or painting the back of the house, she just loved being outdoors and having fun.

'Can I play?' she called out.

Gary waved her away.

‘I’ll be the goalie,’ she said.

‘Fat chance!’ Gary yelled, kicking the ball as hard as he could to prove his point.

‘Oh, go on!’

‘Maybe later,’ her dad said as he ran past.

It was already after five. The light was fading, it would be dark soon and Michelle knew she would miss her chance. Later meant never, or at least not this week or next. It meant when she was big enough to kick the ball as hard as Gary did. And the only way that would ever happen was if she got a chance to practise.

Michelle watched Gary manoeuvre the ball expertly around their dad and down the grass. He made it look so easy and she wanted to see if she could play like that too. He was only 18 months older and wasn’t that much taller than her.

Sick of standing by, she pushed away from the wall and ran out onto the grass, deciding that if they weren’t going to agree to let her play, then she’d just join in like the others did at school. She tried to get close enough to the ball to kick it, but her dad and Gary kept kicking it out of her reach. Then her dad kicked the ball down towards the makeshift goals, tapping it through with his foot.

He did a little victory dance like the professional players did when they scored.

'I'm still winning,' said Gary.

Neither of them seemed to notice that Michelle had joined the game. They were in serious competition, and there wasn't much chance they'd let her be part of it.

She dashed down towards the goal and scooped the ball up from the makeshift jumper goalpost.

'Kick it here,' shouted Gary.

She held it out, as if she was about to drop it and boot it towards him.

'Come on,' Gary said getting impatient.

She knew that as soon as Gary was in control of the ball again, she'd be back to just watching from the side. With a grin, she tucked the ball under her arm, turned towards the house, and sprinted.

'Michelle!' Gary yelled, chasing after her.

Laughing, Michelle banged open the back door and ran inside. Her mum was sitting on the couch as Michelle dashed past the lounge and down the hall towards her room, with Gary hot on her heels.

It wasn't that her mum told her not to play like this, it was just that she didn't quite understand why Michelle wanted to. She had almost made it to

her bedroom when she realised that she wasn't sure why she'd taken the ball in the first place. It wasn't as if she'd be allowed to join in now.

'Gary, don't run through the house in your boots,' Michelle's mum called as Gary sprinted after his sister. The muddy boots would leave marks all over the carpet, and he wasn't supposed to wear them inside.

Groaning, Gary stopped, and started unlacing his boots so he could chase after her in socks. Michelle stopped too. It was too dark to play now so she rolled the ball back down the hallway to her brother, deciding that she'd have to practise without them. One day, she thought, she would be good enough to join in. And she was determined that she would be so good that she'd win!

2
Checkmate

It was Sunday and it had been raining all week. London was grey and miserable, and Michelle was stuck inside again. She'd been hoping to spend the afternoon at Greenwich Park chasing Gary around General Wolfe's statue, but instead they were all cooped up in the warm front room, reading.

Her dad had just finished setting up the chessboard for the daily match. Gary was arguing that it was his turn to be white – white always gets to make the first move. Their dad shrugged. It didn't matter what colour his pieces were, he knew he would always win. He always did. Michelle's dad played competitively, so winning was important to him. He was one of the best chess players in the City of London Police and would sometimes take many months to finish a game playing **postal chess** with his local club.

Postal chess is played the same way as regular chess, except the players play long-distance by marking a card and sending it back and forth through the (snail) mail.

Michelle liked watching because the game was so enticing. She could sit for hours without making any noise. Today, Gary and her dad were sitting cross-legged on the floor and Michelle sat at the end of the low table where they played. She watched as they moved the black and white pieces slowly around the board, taking each other's pawns and knights. Michelle felt a tug of excitement as she figured out why Gary and her dad were making particular moves.

She was used to watching and liked to believe she was invisible. In class at school, she rarely spoke to the teacher, but she took in everything around her. One of her friends joked that Michelle would make a good spy because people sometimes forgot she was there. She liked being overlooked because it meant she could tinker away in her own time, gathering expertise and becoming skilled at something without an audience and then surprise everyone with her new talent.

'Checkmate,' said her dad leaning back with a big grin.

Gary let out a long whistle of breath and reached across to shake their dad's hand. The game was over.

'Can I play?' Michelle asked.

'You? Really?' her dad said.

'Girls don't play chess,' said Gary. 'Not at school anyway.'

Michelle felt a pang of frustration and disappointment in her stomach. It was always the same. She had turned eight a few months before and was tired of always being treated as the one who didn't know things. Sometimes she wanted to show them they were wrong.

'Let's play, Dad,' she said, stealing Gary's spot on the floor as soon as he stood up to go and make a sandwich.

Her dad frowned slightly and grinned. 'You sure?'

'Yes, please.'

'Okay, let's be quick then,' he said.

Michelle was delighted.

It didn't take long to set up the board. Michelle knew where the pieces went and that white always went first. She'd never held the pieces in her hand with the intention to play, but she liked the way the polished wood felt silky smooth beneath her fingers. The set was a big wooden one her dad had bought a long time ago. The base of each piece had felt on the bottom so that it moved smoothly across the board, and the edges were rounded by thousands of games.

'The bishops move diagonally, and the rooks forward and back,' said her dad, as he quickly outlined the rules. But she already knew.

To her father's surprise, Michelle swept her pawn forward and started the game with confidence. Before long she took one of her father's pawns. Up until now he had been busy talking to her mum, but suddenly he was paying attention. She waited for him to retaliate, but instead he moved another one of his pawns forward. She'd watched enough games to know it wasn't always about taking pieces as quickly as possible. It was all about strategy.

Michelle moved her knight out of the back row. She loved the way the knights moved. They could move two squares vertically and one horizontally, or two squares horizontally and one square vertically, in the shape of an L. Most excitingly they could jump other pieces to reach their chosen square.

She knew the knight was a valuable piece, and that it seemed to be the most unpredictable. And that made it her favourite.

The room was quiet while they played, just the soft sounds of the chess pieces being moved across the board. It helped Michelle to think.

Then her mum came into the room with a cup of tea as Michelle took her dad's rook.

'Watch it, Peter, she'll beat you,' said her mum with a chuckle.

Her dad gave a hearty laugh, and then took one of her bishops, a rook, and two pawns. Sensing the change in the game, Michelle edged closer, pushing her long hair out of her face. She was concentrating as hard as she did in her favourite classes at school.

As her parents continued to chat about plans for dinner and whether they should invite the neighbours over before her dad left to do his night shift, Michelle focused on the board. Within just three moves, she could see how to win the game. Her heart raced – could this be true or was it a trick? She knew her dad would likely have seen it too, but he didn't seem to be paying much attention. It was too appealing to ignore. She moved her knight into position. He then moved his rook down the board and took one of her bishops. Instead of seeing her attack, he was in the ruthless mode of just taking her pieces. She waited to see if she had missed something or if he was bluffing. Her excitement grew. She moved her bishop into position, pretending to defend the next piece under attack. After his turn she then moved her queen directly in front of her dad's king. As she took her hand away, she looked up at him.

'Checkmate,' she whispered.

Michelle's mum choked on her tea. Her dad looked back at the board then up at Michelle then back at the board, as if he was trying to work out what had just happened. This time it was Michelle who held out her hand to shake her dad's.

'Beginner's luck,' he said in shock, and then added a little admiringly, 'Good game'.

'Thanks,' said Michelle with a beaming smile.

'You're sure you've never played before?' her dad asked.

'No.'

'Not even at school?' said her mum.

'No.'

'Let's play again,' her dad said, sounding determined.

Michelle understood that her father would now want to play over and over until he'd beaten her many times. She was like him in that way. Competitive. Driven. Beating her father wasn't about winning the game though. It was about proving to him that she could. And then she realised that if her dad didn't think she'd be any good at chess, what else would other people think she wouldn't be good at? It was a thought that intrigued her greatly. How could anyone know what another person is good at, especially when they don't even know themselves.

'I thought you had a lot on, Dad,' said Michelle. 'Aren't you on night duty?'

Michelle's dad was always working on a big case. He worked in one of the busiest police stations in the City of London. It was a miracle if he was home for dinner more than two nights in a row. Michelle liked imagining her dad at work. She loved hearing grabs of conversation about his job, the way he tried to piece things together to stop bad things from happening. She loved even more the few times she'd been allowed to go up to the city and visit him at work.

'I am, but I can't let you think you can beat me!' he chuckled. 'It was just beginner's luck, or perhaps,' he said wryly, as he set up the board again, 'you're a chess champion in the making'.

'Maybe I am,' said Michelle quietly, determined to see if she could beat her father again.

For three hours, they played. Her dad ignored Michelle's mum's questions about getting ready for work or when to have dinner. He didn't speak a word until he'd won the next ten games straight, one after the other. Michelle's head spun from concentrating, and her legs had gone to sleep from sitting on the floor. She leapt up and did some star jumps in the lounge, causing the good china to rattle in the sideboard.

'You read the board well,' he said. 'Another game?'

He had thrown out the challenge. He never held her back when she wanted to learn.

'Can I have dinner first?' Michelle asked lightly. 'I'm starving!'

He laughed. 'Yes, but tomorrow we start.'

3
Hospital visit

It was Saturday afternoon, and Michelle was due to be at a chess tournament in Nottingham. Instead, she was in the car with her mum and dad, heading into St. Thomas's Hospital to see Gary. He'd been in the children's ward for a week and the house was incredibly quiet without him. The doctors were running endless tests, but so far nobody had any answers. All they knew was that Gary had been having trouble seeing, had numerous large lumps developing on his legs and was constantly tired.

Recently, he'd been picked for the junior Tottenham Hotspurs football squad but had barely been able to make a game. It was a huge honour to be selected and it meant Gary was one of the best goalies for his age. Michelle was worried. She knew her brother would do whatever it took to play football, and if he was too sick for that then it had to be something serious.

This was the first time she'd missed a chess tournament in nearly a year. Since beating her dad two years ago, she'd joined the Under 12s London chess club and her weekends were spent playing in tournaments across the country. She was used to sitting down at the table opposite her opponents who would generally smile excitedly when they saw it was a girl they were facing. And then she'd work at slowly beating them.

She played defensively. She placed her pieces strategically so that she built a fortress around her king before commencing her attack. She'd try and consider all possibilities of attack as she built up her armour, and only then would she make her move. Other players were less patient and often reckless, starting an attack before they were ready or trying to remove as many of her pieces as possible. She didn't play like that.

Michelle liked a laugh as much as her friends did, but as soon as she sat behind a chess table, she switched into serious mode. Chess was never something to take lightly. She liked seeing if she could figure out how to win, and loved learning new strategies and moves.

Her dad had offered to let her go to the tournament this weekend and stay with some of the other players because he worried about her missing games. But as much as she loved chess, she wanted to see Gary more. She'd missed him in the house. She would rather be running around outside with him, though, than visiting him in a hospital.

On the way, her dad had to stop in at work and pick something up. They didn't go through the front doors of the police station, instead, going around the back and through the special side doors that only police officers and their families were allowed to use. Two men were coming out as they reached the back door, so they slipped in behind them and found themselves in the stairwell to the top of the scenes-of-crimes part of the station.

Michelle didn't like this part of her dad's work. The stairwell was covered in large black and white crime scene photographs that were gruesome and frightening. They'd been enlarged in the police darkroom and were grainy because they weren't designed to be hanging up on display like an art gallery; they were supposed to be hidden away in a case file down in the basement.

If Gary were with her then he'd make her look at some of the very worst, trying to get her to talk about what she thought might have happened or where the body was in the photo. Once, she and Gary stopped to look at one of a person who had drowned; the image haunted her for days.

Her dad had explained that the photographs were there to remind people about the dangers of being a criminal and the importance of paying attention to detail. Today, Michelle walked as fast as she could without turning her head so she didn't have to catch a glimpse of anything she would later find difficult to forget.

*

After leaving the police station, the three of them drove to the hospital. Her mum was quiet in the front and Michelle knew she was worrying about Gary. They all were.

'We should buy some grapes on the way,' said Michelle. She'd seen someone delivering grapes to a person in hospital on a television show once.

Her mum laughed. 'I don't think Gary likes grapes. What about the latest copy of Beano?'

Beano was a comic that Gary bought sometimes when he'd saved up his pocket money. There was a newsagent stand just near the hospital, so they stopped and bought him a Beano and a packet of Refreshers.

'Do you want some too?' her dad asked, holding out a tube of the chalky, tangy sweets.

'Yes, please!' Michelle didn't have sweets very often and these were one of her favourites.

As they headed up the stairs into St. Thomas's, the huge London hospital, Michelle felt her stomach drop. Up until now, she hadn't given too much thought to where Gary was, but this felt real. It smelled like cleaning products and fear, and she stepped a little closer to her dad.

She sucked on one of the sweets as they walked upstairs and down corridors until they reached the children's ward. Gary was at the very end, and Michelle tried not to look at the faces of the other occupants, treating it a little like she did when she walked past the crime scene photos. She looked at the ground and then up to find Gary.

He was in a bed under a grimy window, looking small lying there, as if he'd shrunk over the past few days. She handed him the Refreshers and the copy of Beano. He gave her a weak smile and said hello.

Her mum kissed him on the head. The doctor came and asked her parents to step outside so he could update them on what they had found out.

Michelle watched them walk out of the ward, leaving her alone with Gary. She was very excited to see him.

'Have you talked to any of the other kids?' Michelle asked. Usually, her brother was outgoing and made friends easily.

He shook his head. 'Not really. We just sort of keep to ourselves. And it looks like I'm going to miss my end-of-school exams,' he said, looking miserable.

'Oh,' she said, feeling awful for him.

'The doctors still don't know what's wrong with me, so they're keeping me in for more tests, and the exams are next week.'

She knew Gary wanted to go to the local grammar school with his friends, but if he didn't sit the exams, he might not get in.

'I bet you'll be home by then,' said Michelle lightly.

Gary looked across at her and she noticed the dark rings under his eyes. 'They keep taking blood every day, but I don't think they've found anything.'

Gary always had energy. More than anyone she'd ever met. She couldn't even remember seeing him lie on the couch with a cold for more than an hour. Michelle tore the end of his packet of Refreshers. 'Here, you love these.'

He let her drop a sweet into his hand and he popped it in his mouth. It made her feel a little better watching him chew it.

'Trade you the green one?' Gary asked, holding out one of the sweets from the tube. He hated lime flavour. Michelle wasn't a fan either, but she couldn't really refuse her brother. Not today.

She swapped him an orange one and he popped it in his mouth. There was something about eating sweets together that made it feel as if they were home and not in a hospital.

'Are you missing chess this weekend?' Gary asked.

Michelle nodded. 'I'm going to the park later,' she said, and then instantly regretted it. 'Sorry.'

'It's okay. You should be outside. Make up for me being stuck in here!'

But she still felt guilty that she was doing normal things while he was sick. She tried to talk to him about Arsenal, but it was obvious he just wanted to sleep.

By the time her parents had returned with some plastic cups of milky looking tea, Gary was already asleep.

'Mum, is he going to be okay?' Michelle whispered.

Her mum tried a small smile but had a distant look in her eyes. She swallowed hard and Michelle knew immediately that whatever news they'd had was not good.

Her dad patted her on the shoulder. 'He'll be here a while, love.'

'For the weekend?'

'For the week. Maybe longer,' said her dad.

'Oh,' said Michelle, feeling hopeless. 'Then I'd better leave him my sweets too.'

She took them from her pocket and left them near the copy of the Beano on his bedside hospital table. She didn't know what else to do.

*

It had been weeks, but Gary was finally coming home from hospital. He had a diagnosis of Behçet's syndrome which Michelle didn't fully understand, but she knew it was grim. They'd established that it was a rare blood disease, and her parents had been told that he probably wouldn't live until adulthood. He was one of the youngest kids to have ever been diagnosed with this disease and it meant years and years of drugs. Michelle was still in shock but found it too hard to think about. It was too overwhelming to imagine her big brother not being around.

She'd missed him madly whilst he was in hospital and was so relieved that he was coming home. He'd missed the entrance exams and most of his Arsenal games, but he would soon be back in the house, cracking jokes and talking football.

Her mum had been very **stoic**, clearly worried about Gary and his future, but determined to ensure he would have a happy life. She'd overheard her parents talking about how they wanted him to have all the experiences he could, to make up for whatever was going to happen.

Stoic: determined not to complain or show your feelings, especially when something bad happens to you.

Because he'd missed the exams it meant he couldn't get a place at the grammar school, so he was off to the big comprehensive school at the edge of their catchment area. Michelle was going to sit the exams in a year or so. She was hoping she could go to the local girl's grammar school instead of the comprehensive where it was rumoured that fights broke out on an hourly basis.

'No sticking your fingers in the icing,' said Michelle's mum as she finished spreading the rich chocolate icing across the top of the cake that she'd made for Gary's homecoming.

Michelle smiled, knowing it would be the first thing her brother would do when he walked in. Michelle's mum had been rushing around all morning cleaning the house and making Gary's bed. Michelle knew she was trying to make things nice for him, but she also knew he probably wouldn't notice if his sheets were clean, or the carpets had been vacuumed.

'Gary needs a lot of rest. Don't go getting him all excited,' said her mum.

Before she could answer, they both heard the car pull up outside. Michelle rushed to the window to see her dad helping her brother climb out. Gary looked different since she'd visited him in the hospital, as if he'd been pumped up with fluid.

Michelle opened the front door and ran out onto the street. It was only when she was dashing across the cold, wet grass that she realised she'd forgotten to put on her shoes. Her socks were damp within seconds, and she bounced around on the cold grass.

Gary grinned at her, and even though he looked pale and tired, he still looked like her lovely, big brother. 'Where are your shoes, you duffer?'

Michelle shrugged, dancing around him as he walked slowly towards the house, letting their dad bring in the bags. She wanted to hug him, but she wasn't sure if that would hurt him or not. She still didn't really understand how it felt to have a rare blood disease. She'd been trying to research it at school but there was nothing in the library.

'Mum made cake!' Michelle said.

'I should hope so,' said Gary.

'You can probably even lick the icing!'

'Can I get inside first?'

Michelle realised she was slowing him down, and she moved aside so their mum could hug him gently in the doorway. Michelle heard her mum speak reassuring words to Gary as he went in, giving him a big squeeze and gently putting her arm around his shoulders.

Gary shuffled inside and headed straight for the cake. Michelle watched as he slid his finger across the top edge, gathered a large clump of icing and stuck it in his mouth. She waited for their mum to say something, but instead she just laughed.

Michelle poked her finger into the icing too, but instead of laughing, her mum swotted away her hand.

'Not fair!' Michelle said.

Gary grinned at her, and Michelle found she didn't mind at all that she couldn't lick the top of the cake. She was just happy to have her brother home.

4
Chess champion

Michelle was awake before her alarm because of the butterflies in her stomach. It seemed as if she'd been waiting for this day forever, but given she was only ten it hadn't been all that long. Today was the London Primary Schools' Chess Association Tournament and she'd been selected to represent her school.

It wasn't just that she'd been chosen to play, it was that she'd won many games to get to this point and hadn't lost a game in ages. Since first beating her dad when she was eight, Michelle discovered that she was rather skilled at playing chess. She'd since won many tournaments and championships, and even some trophies. Her brother Gary was right about girls not playing chess though, because there were very few at the tournaments.

Michelle had practised hard for months for today's tournament, playing her dad and even Gary, nearly every day. They could both still usually outplay her, but she was winning more and more games against them.

She opened the curtains to a sunny morning and dressed as fast as she could. She'd had an extra-long bath the night before and had hung her clothes in her cupboard so there would be no creases.

Her dad had arranged to have the day off work just so he could watch, and Gary was coming too. She didn't want to lose. She didn't want to let them down. She had half hoped that nobody would be there to see her play, because it made it very real having an audience. But she knew there would be a crowd. Other players and teachers and parents.

She'd played in tournaments before but nothing as important as this one. Held in central London in a large, impressive building, there were hundreds of players from schools across the country. She was competing in the Under 12s, and she'd be up against other students who had made chess their lives.

Michelle's dad was always up before her mum. 'I thought you might like a proper breakfast,' he said as she walked into the kitchen. The smell of bacon frying made her stomach turn.

'I'm not hungry, Dad.'

'You must eat something. That brain of yours needs feeding,' he said, dishing up a mountain of eggs, sausages and bacon that would feed about four families.

Michelle sat at the table, watching her mum clean up around them. She always did a million jobs at once before going off to work as the manager of a local bank.

'Are you nervous, Mickeydoo?' Her mum asked using the nickname given to her by her grandmother, Hessie.

Michelle nodded. 'A little.'

'Don't be. You'll be fine.'

'I don't want to let Dad down,' Michelle said.

'Then eat up,' said her mum. 'You won't get much time for a break today. Not until after. You don't want to be thinking about your growling stomach.'

Michelle laughed and picked a crispy slice of bacon from the plate. She chewed the end but didn't really want it. She couldn't stop worrying about what everyone would think if she lost.

'You can't eat all that. Shove over,' said Gary, sliding down next to her. She happily let him share her plate of breakfast, pleased she didn't have to eat it all. Gary was always hungry and had been putting on weight since he'd left hospital. He'd even been trying to practise football again.

'Stop stealing her food,' said Michelle's mum.

'She's too nervous to eat,' said Gary winking at Michelle. He always knew how she was really feeling.

'It's true. I'm going to get ready,' she said, heading to her room before anyone could stop her.

If she won today, Michelle knew it would make her dad happy. However, it would also increase the chance that everyone would expect her to continue playing more often, and even consider chess as a career. She knew that meant hours and hours of practice and playing championships across the country. While she loved playing chess, deep down she also wanted to do other things with her time. Like playing sport or painting or dancing.

She sat on her bed and looked around her small, neat room. It was a **box room**, with no frills. She added another clip to her hair, making sure it would not work its way out of the ponytail. Now she just had to hurry along her dad and brother so they could get to the championships on time.

Box room: small room in some British houses normally used for storage but sometimes used as a bedroom.

An hour and twenty-three minutes later, Michelle walked up the stairs outside the town hall. She couldn't believe the crowds. There were banners hanging from the roof and kids everywhere.

Sensing her nerves, her dad took her hand. 'Come on. Let's use police tactics and manoeuvre our way through.'

'It's called pushing,' said Gary as they weaved through the crowds to the front where the registration table stood. As Michelle gave her name and school details to the woman sitting at the desk, she looked surprised because there were no other girls registered, and she checked if Gary was playing too.

The games were set up at a series of tables in the large hall. The familiar smell of plastic chess pieces and wooden boards filled the room. Onlookers were watching on either side in large, tiered seating. Gary and her dad wished her luck as she went to find her first game.

It was at table 12 against a boy called Ian who was wearing a brown school uniform. He didn't look nervous at all as she sat down opposite him. There was a referee whose job it was to watch the game and ensure they pushed the button on the clock after each turn so the players didn't take too long for their moves.

Michelle tried to block out the noise around her as Ian picked up his first piece. Sometimes she liked to play slowly and cautiously, while other times it felt as if the pieces spoke to her, and then she moved swiftly through the game.

Ian was a confident player, but he made a mistake early on when he left his queen open to attack. Michelle swept in with her rook, and the game was over in a matter of minutes. She'd won round one.

Between her games, Michelle watched some of the other players. She tried to observe as much as she could about their weaknesses so that if she came to play them during the day, she would know how to win.

Her second game was against a tall, lanky boy who had to tuck his legs up under his chair because there wasn't room for him to stretch out. He was a more thoughtful player than Ian, and the game took much longer.

After each game she'd look across to the stands to see her dad and Gary. Her dad would give her a little nod of encouragement and Gary would grin with excitement. Michelle kept winning. Game after game. Until it was time for the final.

Her opponent, Jamie, was small and dark-haired and she'd noticed him watching her earlier in the day. They shook hands, and he went first. The hall was silent. Within four moves, Michelle knew this game was different. She could sense the boy trying to read her play. So instead of using one of the openings she'd memorised, she changed her game.

Taking his pieces as swiftly as she could, she played aggressively. He sat up straighter in his chair and she watched him scan the board. She kept her body still, trying to calm the waves of emotion that sometimes came when she was most trying to win.

Then it was her turn. She reached for her bishop. She was planning to move it towards the boy's rook, readying to take his piece, and was about to touch it when she saw another move, a much better one.

Switching tactics, she grabbed her knight from where it was waiting to be put to action. It was still her favourite piece. As she looked up, she saw the boy frown at her move. She'd thrown him off, which was what she'd wanted.

Three moves later she said, 'Checkmate'.

The boy stared down at the board trying to find a way out, but she knew he couldn't. She had his king covered. She'd won.

The boy shook her hand, his fingers sweaty. He mumbled congratulations and she thanked him. She was the new Chess Champion in her age group.

After much clapping, an organiser manoeuvred her to the podium for the ceremony. There were a lot of people around filling in forms and bustling about. She was asked onto the podium with the other winners and was handed her trophy, a certificate and her prize. She had won a set of three chess books by famous chess players, on opening moves and strategies.

She scanned the crowd for her dad and Gary and found them grinning and waving. It was a big day for her family, and for her. She was very happy not to have let anyone down. While the awards continued around her, Michelle glanced down at the certificate and read the words:

MICHELLE SIMMONS WAS SELECTED TO PLAY FOR HIS SCHOOL IN 1977 AND HIS PERFORMANCE WAS HIGHLY CREDITABLE.

Michelle was very amused that the organisers had only printed certificates assuming that the participants and winners would all be boys. Knowing that made winning even better.

5
Chess, chess and more chess

Michelle's dad had big plans for her chess career, wanting to see if she could become a **grandmaster**, but she wasn't too sure that she felt the same way. She loved playing chess. She loved the thrill of building an army, making a strong defence, and then attacking, trying to read her opponent and work out their strategy. She also enjoyed the experience of being overlooked for just being a girl and then winning. But...

Grandmaster: the highest title a chess player can have and it takes thousands of hours of chess, dedication, and talent. They hold the title for life.

To be a grandmaster meant dedicating everything to chess. It meant staying inside all weekend and practising, never playing netball or football, not seeing her other friends or family and missing out on hours of fun. And Michelle just wasn't sure she could do that.

Last week, her dad had taken her to see someone who assessed and graded young chess players. The man had studied her previous games and played Michelle for a couple of hours. After testing her, he told her father that Michelle had the potential to be a grandmaster.

Her dad had bubbled over with pride. He could barely contain himself on the car trip home and wanted to tell everyone. Michelle was not so keen. It was something that many of her chess friends wanted. To be good enough. But she also lived in fear for what it meant for the rest of her life.

She had improved enormously since the first time she played, and rarely lost a game. But instead of feeling great about her winning streak, she'd started worrying about what would happen if she lost. How could she let her father down? She didn't like that feeling very much. Sometimes she stared out the window during a tournament, longing to be outside in the fresh air.

Today she was visiting her chess friend, Nigel, who played for the same team. He'd been playing chess pretty much since the day he could walk.

Nigel lived in London, too, but quite far away, so she had never been to his house. He was quirky and highly competitive, but Michelle liked the fact that he teased her about losing and about the face she pulled sometimes when she was concentrating the hardest. She was sort of hoping that Nigel would help give her inspiration, because he loved chess much more than she did.

Michelle's dad and Nigel's dad got along well too, and they were three cups of tea into a conversation when Michelle and Nigel asked if they could leave the room and go up the narrow-winding stairs to Nigel's room for a game.

Nigel stopped at the top of the stairs with his hand on the door. 'You ready?'

'Ready to beat you? Of course!' she said laughing.

He shook his head. 'No, I mean are you ready to see the wonder?'

Michelle wasn't sure what he was talking about, so she just shrugged and then nodded. Nigel gave a little flourish as he pushed open his bedroom door and stood aside so she could see his room. 'Ta da!'

Michelle stared. She didn't know what to say. She was astonished and amazed.

'Wow!' she finally said.

His bedroom was one giant chess set. The walls were black and white squares. The bedspread was a black-and-white chequered chess board. On the wall there were shelves full of well-thumbed chess books. Even the rug on the floor was a giant black knight. And right in the middle of the room was a wooden table with a chess board permanently set up.

'Do you like it?' Nigel said, pushing into the room.

'If I didn't know you liked chess before, then I sure would now,' said Michelle lightly.

'I don't just like chess. I live for chess,' said Nigel.

'Oh…,' said Michelle.

'Don't you?'

She thought about it for a second. If living for chess meant her bedroom had to look like this, then no. She preferred her white **duvet** (doona) cover, with small pink and blue flowers.

'I'm not sure,' she said finally.

'But you're such a good player,' said Nigel. 'One day this will be you.'

He waved towards the bookshelf full of biographies of famous chess players and books on chess strategies. She'd read a couple of them in the school library, but the only ones she owned were the three she'd won in the championship. She scanned the spines of the books for some that weren't about chess, but couldn't seem to find any.

'Have you read all of these?' Michelle asked.

'Of course. Haven't you?'

Feeling a little overwhelmed, Michelle shook her head. 'No.'

'You should.' Nigel went to pull one of the books out of the shelves. 'They really teach you how to win.'

He slid a thick, heavy book out and held it up. 'This one? Amazing. It's about Kasparov. You can borrow it. If you promise to give it back.'

Michelle knew that Kasparov was a famous Russian grandmaster and a champion player, but that didn't mean she wanted to read a book about him. 'Oh, it's okay. You keep it – I might lose it,' she said.

Nigel nodded as if he understood and pushed the book back onto the shelf. Michelle looked around the room trying to find something that suggested Nigel had other interests. But it was all chess. There wasn't even a teddy on his bed. She realised that as much as she enjoyed playing, she certainly didn't care enough about it to spend all her time living and breathing chess. Not like this.

'Maybe we should just play,' she said.

Michelle took the black side of the table to be polite because it was Nigel's house, sitting with her knees squashed under the edge. She was taller than Nigel and felt a little like Alice in the looking glass after she'd had the drink-me potion.

Nigel moved his pawn. Michelle followed. She was pleased he didn't use the timer they sometimes used in tournaments. Maybe this could be a friendlier game.

'Are you going away over the holidays?' Michelle asked, trying to make conversation.

Nigel shook his head. 'No time.'

Michelle knew that some of the others on the team took chess very seriously, but she hadn't realised that Nigel was so committed to it. She was looking forward to the days her family spent at the beach. It meant fish and chips and swimming in the sea.

'I have my evaluation in January,' said Nigel. 'To find out if I'm good enough.'

Michelle nodded as Nigel took her pawn. She knew what he was playing but for some reason she wasn't that interested in the game.

'I had mine last week.'

Nigel stopped staring at the board and looked at her. 'And?'

She nodded to indicate that the news had been good.

'I knew you were talented enough,' he said.

'Thanks. I didn't.'

'Wow. Your whole life is going to be perfect now.'

Michelle laughed at how serious he sounded. 'Is it? Chess isn't the only thing I like doing.'

'It is for me. I'm going to play for England and it's all I want to do'.

Michelle picked up her knight, remembering back to the very first game she had with her father when she'd beaten him without having played before. The knight was still her favourite piece, but the more Nigel talked about his love of the game, the more Michelle wondered what would be the one thing that would make her so passionate, that would make her decorate her bedroom like this. Because she now knew for certain that it wasn't going to be chess.

6
Eltham Green Comprehensive

It had been a year since Michelle had broken the news to her dad that she was giving up her chess career. He had tried everything to talk her out of quitting the team. She knew it was difficult for him to accept her decision. He'd already jumped ahead to her being a grandmaster, so he was having a hard time readjusting.

Michelle didn't even want to play socially anymore. It just felt as if the game had left her head. Last week she'd sat her scholarship exams and been offered a place at the local girl's grammar school, Blackheath High. But since Gary had missed his entrance exams when he was in hospital, their parents had decided that Michelle shouldn't accept the scholarship, because they wanted their children to be at school together.

This meant that when school started in September, Michelle would be wearing the dark green uniform of Eltham Green Comprehensive. She didn't really mind. At least she'd be walking to school or catching the bus with her brother.

'It's not like being at primary school,' said Gary. 'It's a bit like a jungle.'

Michelle was sitting on the hard chair next to his hospital bed. Gary had been back in hospital for the past month. Michelle was very happy to visit him, and he seemed really pleased to see her.

'Some of the kids are wild!' He raised an eyebrow as if he was trying to shock her.

'And then there's Mr Dawson,' he said with a smile.

They were sharing a packet of crisps and Michelle had left all the crumbs for Gary. He drained them into his mouth in one gulp.

'Who's Mr Dawson?'

'The headmaster. The rumour is that he's the toughest headmaster in the whole of Britain.'

Michelle swallowed hard. Her primary school had been sweet and caring and nothing like the comprehensive sounded.

'Apparently, he used to be a boxer and he's been punched in the face so many times his nose is all broken and he can't smell properly.'

Michelle laughed. Her brother was obviously trying to scare her.

'It's true. His nickname is Batman because he wears a black academic gown that looks like a cape. He stands on the roof of the main building at lunch with his binoculars glued to his face, watching for fights in the playground. If he sees anyone fighting, then they get called to his office on the Tannoy system and punished.'

'What's a Tannoy system?' Michelle asked.

Gary explained that it was a public broadcasting system with speakers in each of the classrooms and in the corridors.

'There are heaps of fights at lunchtime, but just keep your head down and you'll get used to it,' said Gary, picking up the other packet of crisps and tearing them open. Michelle always brought crisps to the hospital because Gary said the food was tasteless.

'Can we talk about something else now?' she asked. 'You're making it sound awful!'

'I can tell you about the boy who was expelled.'

'Go on,' said Michelle.

'His name is George O'Dowd. He used to wear a bin liner to school instead of a school blazer.

The headmaster never really liked him because sometimes he wore makeup, and he'd sing all the time,' he said.

'What happened to him?' Michelle asked.

'He always used to bunk off school, then one day, he disappeared. Never came back. Everyone says he's set up a band.'

The nurse arrived, interrupting them to give her brother his medication. Michelle knew she had to leave, but first asked Gary what flavour crisps he wanted when she visited the following week. Smiling, he told her to get one of each. Before the nurse could start to take his blood again, Michelle scurried out of the ward. She still didn't like to think of her big brother being sick and also, she knew he hated his blood being taken.

*

It wasn't long before Gary was back home, and it was Michelle's first day at Eltham Green Comprehensive. Together they set off, walking the three miles (almost 5 km) to school, passing their grandparents' place on the way. There wasn't time to stop in for a cup of tea because Michelle was keen to see her new school.

As they got closer, she let herself be dragged along in the tide of other students walking in. It was noisy and busy. She took a deep breath as she saw the huge building for the first time. Shaped like an enormous 'H' it was nicknamed 'H-block' after a popular TV show about a large prison in Britain.

Eltham Green Comprehensive was one of the newer inner London government schools that was designed to educate large numbers of students. It was a massive concrete and brick compound with big windows in the middle of a large block of fields, with more than 2000 students marching across the paths towards the entrance.

‘Come on, trouble,’ said her brother. ‘This way.’

Michelle followed her brother. She didn’t know where she was going, just that Gary had told her to follow the hordes. Gary had warned her about the bleeps that marked the end of lessons that were broadcast through the speakers. He’d told her that depending on which classroom you were in, they could be crackly and out-of-tune or far too loud, making everyone jump from the fright of hearing the noise.

Some of Michelle’s friends from her primary school were also going to the comprehensive, and she was looking out for them while trying not to bump into anyone, which might start a fight. Last night she’d dreamt that the school was just a big riot zone, but now she was here, it seemed calmer than she’d expected.

‘Assembly Hall is down the corridor at the back of the main building. That’s where you have to go,’ said Gary as they pushed through the steel and glass doors into the school.

‘There are two lifts, but don’t use them. Just take the stairs with everyone else. There are only five floors, and the lifts are not for students,’ he continued. ‘You’ll have to walk hundreds of flights of stairs a week so go fast and don't let anyone push you over or bang into you.'

Michelle nodded. It was all so overwhelming. She tried to look for others who seemed as lost as she did. The corridor floor was chequered with black-and-white squares that reminded her of an old chessboard. It somehow made her relax as she hurried along with the tide towards the end of one of the buildings.

'There's the Assembly Hall,' said Gary, pointing to the big open double doors. A stream of students was being waved in by a teacher. 'You good?' he asked.

'Yeah, think so.'

'I've got football practice, so I'll see you later.' He headed off down the corridor with his bag hanging from one shoulder.

She turned and headed for the doors of the hall. It was an impressive building, with high ceilings and hundreds of chairs in rows across the parquetry floor. She found a seat on the end of a row next to a girl who looked as overwhelmed as she felt.

The girl smiled as Michelle sat down, tugging on her uniform. Michelle took her first proper breath for the morning, as the headmaster walked onto the stage and began to speak. His voice was loud and firm as he explained how the school operated. All Michelle could think of was his broken nose which did look as mushed as Gary said it did.

*

It wasn't long before trouble found her. One of the girls from her primary school, Stacey, had also come to Eltham Green. Unlike Michelle, Stacey wasn't keen on learning and had formed a gang that was notorious for terrorising the new girls in the year.

One day as they were walking down the five flights of stairs from the science class, Stacey pushed Michelle hard, causing her to fall. Pulling herself up, Michelle confronted the girl.

'What was that for?' she asked.

Stacey looked flustered for a moment and then realising that everyone was watching her, spat out, 'bottom gate, 3.30'.

Michelle knew it meant a fight at the end of the day at the lowest gate. This was the last thing Michelle wanted. She had been taught to avoid fights and to walk away from trouble. But everyone had heard the challenge and it wasn't long before the whole school knew.

That afternoon, as she walked towards the bottom gate, she could hear the crowds. Hundreds of students had gathered, buzzing to watch the fight. In the middle of the crowd was Stacey, surrounded by her gang. Michelle, not quite knowing what to do, dropped her school bag and walked straight up to her.

'Right then,' said Michelle, waiting to see what would happen.

Stacey clenched her knuckles, flashing large rings on her fingers that resembled knuckle dusters. Michelle did not want to get hit by a fistful of those. As Stacey swung her right fist towards Michelle's face, Michelle instinctively grabbed it, preventing the hit from landing. Michelle was much bigger than Stacey, so it was easy for her to grip Stacey's hand tightly and stop any more blows. For a minute, they stood there staring at each other.

And then suddenly, Stacey pulled hard, wriggled her hand free and ran off into the crowd who separated in surprise. Michelle waited to see if the other members of the gang would come after her, but once Stacey left, they all turned and fled. Disappointed that the fight was over, even the crowd started to leave.

Michelle picked up her bag and set off home. As she rounded the corner, she found Stacey sitting on a wall crying.

'I looked pathetic,' she said. 'No one will ever take me seriously again.'

Michelle found herself feeling sorry for the girl who was constantly in trouble, even in primary school.

'Don't worry,' she said, putting her arm around Stacey's shoulders. 'Everyone will forget soon enough; there are plenty of other fights to keep them occupied.'

And from that day on Michelle was never challenged to a fight again. Instead, she spent hours sitting on the wall around the corner from the bottom gate, chatting with her best friend, Arvinder. Arvinder was wickedly witty and could make Michelle laugh more than anyone.

*

The months at Eltham Green Comprehensive passed by quickly, with Michelle throwing herself into all her classes. On the weekends she would go into Covent Garden with Arvinder to shop and watch movies. One night Gary, Michelle and her mum were sitting watching the TV, and saw a large, bright yellow van in the background of a BBC news story about a hostage siege at the Iranian Embassy in London. The van was distinctive and similar to the one nicknamed the 'yellow peril', that was usually parked in their driveway. Michelle had never been allowed in it.

'Hey, that's Dad's van!' Gary said, pointing at the television.

Michelle and her mum stared in disbelief. It couldn't be. Why would his van be outside the embassy? Michelle had always thought of her dad as a London bobby, in uniform, walking London streets, catching crooks and getting kittens out of trees. But she'd never actually seen him in a bobby uniform.

Over the next six days the three of them remained glued to the TV as the siege intensified. It was a big news story. Twenty-six hostages were taken, people had died, and lots of London police were involved.

When her dad finally returned home, Michelle really wanted to ask him about his involvement in the siege, but she waited until they'd finished dinner before she worked up the courage to raise the subject.

'Dad, were you at the Iranian Embassy during the siege?'

He looked at her from over the top of the newspaper. She waited for him to spin a story as he normally did, but instead, he nodded. And returned to his paper.

Michelle left the tea towel on the bench, knowing the dishes would dry anyway in the rack, and moved to the chair opposite her dad. She never let conversations slip away if she was close to the truth.

'Did you help free the hostages, Dad?'

'I'm just reading about Arsenal. Can we talk about this later?'

'We saw your van on the telly outside the embassy.' She thought perhaps her dad would be more likely to tell her the truth if he knew that they knew.

'How did you know it was mine? Must be hundreds of those vans in London.'

'Not with that number plate! We all recognised it.'

Her dad smiled as he lowered the paper. 'You'd all make good detectives.'

She shook her head. 'No, I don't think I'd like to solve crimes. I like building things and pulling them apart. But I do want to hear about the siege.'

Ever since she quit chess, her dad was always trying to work out what she'd be when she finished school. He'd only accepted that she wasn't going to become a grandmaster because she told him there was something else out there that would make her even more determined and excited.

'Well, I'm a detective in the crime squad. Can't talk about the siege because it's still live. But yes, I was there. And I'd like to think that I helped.'

'I always thought you were a bobby,' said Michelle lightly.

Her dad smiled. 'I look ridiculous in those tall helmets!'

Michelle laughed. 'Doesn't everyone?'

Michelle left her dad to his paper and went into her room to think about the fact that he was much more interesting than she'd ever realised. And it made her wonder what other things she'd overlooked.

*

Despite the constant distractions of the fights in class and in the playground, Michelle loved her school. She loved listening to her teachers explain theories and ideas that she'd never thought about before. She was torn between an equal love of literature, history and science.

History meant hours of stories about the world and about the kings and queens of England. Elizabeth I, the Queen of England from 1558 to 1603, was her favourite because although she'd been third in line to the throne behind her younger brother Edward and elder half-sister Mary, she became Queen when she was only 25, after her siblings had both died. Michelle was fascinated by the idea of this young monarch who had everything stacked against her, who was in constant fear for her life, and who ruled for nearly 50 years.

She tried to imagine a time when female rulers were so rare, and where, if Elizabeth had said something wrong or didn't handle a situation successfully, then her enemies would take control and she could be beheaded. And yet Elizabeth had survived, thrived as a leader, and kept the country going strong for decades. She had been an inspiring speaker and people admired her.

Michelle, however, hated speaking in public. She had become a master at avoiding speaking up in class. In her English literature class, she'd figured out how to change seats each lesson so that she was never next in line to read. She'd managed to get through almost an entire year without saying anything other than, 'here', when the roll was called.

But just because she wasn't speaking up, it didn't mean that she wasn't constructing all sorts of opinions in her head. At home she'd talk to her mum about things, and also seek out Gary to talk about teachers and other students; and if he was back in hospital then she'd store up all the stories for when she visited him each weekend.

She knew that the hardest thing for her would be narrowing down her path to one passion. And just as she'd had to say goodbye to her chess career, soon she would have to think about specialising in one area.

7
Building the ZX81

The house was still full of decorations from the weekend. Balloons bobbed in Arsenal colours across the ceiling and streamers hung from the doors. It had been Gary's fifteenth birthday party and he'd invited a few more than the ten friends his parents had suggested. Their dad had to make several trips to the chippie down the road for more fish and chips because Gary's football friends ate so much.

Usually, birthdays in the Simmons' household were small events with family and maybe a couple of friends if it was a special one. But Michelle knew that their parents wouldn't have minded if Gary had invited the whole borough because this birthday had been a big deal. The doctors had always said that Gary probably wouldn't make it to 15, and he liked telling anyone who would listen that the doctors were wrong.

He'd had one of his longest stretches away from hospital and was feeling well enough to be back playing football with his mates. Michelle and Gary's parents had given him a Sinclair ZX81 for his birthday – a new form of personal computer that had just been released – and Gary was one of the first people at school to have one.

It had just arrived in a box in kit form with pages of detailed instructions, which meant Gary had to spend hours building it. Michelle knew that putting all the parts together, and then getting it to work, was surely the most exciting aspect.

As soon as he'd walked in from school, Gary had covered his bedroom floor with computer parts. Michelle knew how keen he was to get started because he hadn't eaten the 19 sandwiches he'd usually polish off before dinner. Instead, he'd just dropped his bag, opened the box, and started.

Now he had the soldering iron in one hand, a pair of old plastic lab glasses on his face and was methodically working his way through attaching various elements to the motherboard.

'My fingers are smaller than yours. You sure you don't want help?' Michelle asked for the hundredth time that afternoon.

Gary made a sound like a growl which she took to mean no. Disappointed, she returned to pulling apart her bike. She was only pulling it apart because she wasn't allowed to help build the computer. She'd pulled her bike apart a few times over the past year, and it was easy. She finished tightening the front brakes, wondering if that would make her braking more effective on the big hill near home.

'Why isn't this working?' exclaimed Gary in exasperation, dropping the soldering iron onto his desk.

'Do you want me to have a look?' Michelle asked quietly.

He glanced across at her. She was spinning the front wheel to check it was aligned properly. 'You finished already?'

She nodded. 'Yep.'

'Better get your bike out of the house before Mum gets home, then.'

'So, you do want my help,' Michelle said playfully.

'No. Don't need it.'

Smiling to herself, Michelle lifted her bike so that it was the right way up and wheeled it through the kitchen and out the back door. She was desperate to have a go on Gary's computer. She didn't just want to help him fix it, she wanted to see how it worked.

She leaned her bike up against the back of the house and hurried inside. Gary was bent over the soldering iron so she couldn't see what part he was attaching. Hating being excluded, she lent in as close as she could, her head almost bumping against his shoulder.

'You're too close,' he said.

'You sure that's right?' she asked him.

'Michelle!'

She started giggling, unable to help herself. It wasn't very often that Gary lost his cool but when he did it was more amusing than anything.

'Honestly, one day I'm going to buy you a one-way ticket to Australia!' Gary said.

'You'd miss me too much,' she told him.

He rolled his eyes. Perhaps it was because he'd spent so much time in hospital and she was always worrying about him that they got along well, particularly compared to some of her friends who fought with their brothers.

'Okay. You can solder one tiny bit. Then that's it!' Gary said, handing her the iron. He pointed out exactly what she needed to do, but she'd already worked that out. She'd read over the instructions when he was setting up.

Holding the iron still, she got started soldering the components. She knew Gary was watching her closely, but she felt confident doing this sort of work. Her hand was steady, and she was precise about the way she worked. She'd read that most faults on the kit were due to bad soldering, so she had to make sure her job was perfect.

She stood up as she finished, although she really wanted to keep going. She looked across at Gary, trying to gauge what he thought. He groaned again, and then nodded, telling her silently she could start work attaching the next part.

'Don't think this means you're going to get to use the computer when it's finished.'

'I won't.'

She attached the next component and gave Gary back the soldering iron but told him she'd stay and hand him the rest of the larger pieces as if he was a surgeon. He laughed.

It took a couple of hours for them to finish assembling the ZX81, but neither of them wanted to stop. They knew they had to try and get it done before dinner.

'We just need to check if there're any missing bits,' said Gary, peering close to the board.

Michelle liked the way he included her in this. 'Looks pretty good to me.'

'Time to test if it works.'

Gary plugged the keyboard tails into the connectors. Then he connected the computer to the power supply. They waited a second.

'It works!' Gary exclaimed excitedly. 'We did it!'

'We really did!'

Michelle helped him to fit the case around the computer. It was fiddly and hard, and she was sure there must be a simpler way to build something like this. They had to screw the case in with tiny screws, so Gary was happy to let Michelle have a go.

When they were finished, they had to move the computer to Gary's desk because there was no way their parents would allow it to sit on the floor for a minute longer than necessary.

'Okay, you take that end,' said Gary. 'We need to go really slowly.'

Michelle slid her hands under the edge of the case. She waited for Gary to tell her to lift before they carried the computer across the room together. He'd already cleared his desk, so they slid it on as gently as they could.

'Thanks for your help,' said Gary. 'You're pretty good at this.'

She didn't say anything even though she knew he was right. She was pretty good at this kind of stuff. Maybe one day she'd build her own computer.

8
Flying to the moon

It had been challenging for Michelle to choose her subjects for her **A-levels.** She loved humanities subjects like history and literature, but she also loved the sciences like physics, chemistry and biology. She'd talked it over with friends from school, but most of them were more interested in picking the subjects with the least work. None of them were that keen to do A-levels in the first place because they weren't as committed to going to university as she was. She'd realised a while back that she was different from a lot of the other students at Eltham Green. She liked to learn, and she found the endless disruptions from some of the other kids in her class frustrating because it stopped the teachers from teaching.

A-levels: in England and Wales entrance to universities depends on the results from these final-year exams – similar to our ATAR score.

That night, Michelle waited for her dad to get home from work. She'd already decided to try and talk through her subject choices with him because she knew he'd be honest and push her as hard as he did when she showed talent with chess.

'Cup of tea, Dad?'

He looked up and nodded. She went into the kitchen and took down the finest china cups and made a proper pot, heating them first and then letting the tea steep for three minutes before carrying them out on a tray to the lounge.

'You play mother,' said her dad.

Michelle smiled, finding the expression funny and old-fashioned. She knew that it meant that she had to pour the tea into the cups and add his sugar. As she did, her dad folded the paper and lay it down next to him on the arm of the chair. Michelle noticed an advertisement in colour that ran across half the page.

BRITISH ASTRONAUTS WANTED.

NO EXPERIENCE NECESSARY.

Michelle's dad noticed what she was reading. 'An astronaut, hey?'

She shrugged as if it meant nothing, but she'd thought about it once or twice. They'd talked about space travel at school, and she was taken with the idea of going somewhere new and travelling for a purpose. She imagined the enormous pressure that astronauts would be under, and she liked that aspect as well. She wanted a job where things mattered, where life wasn't just easy.

'Imagine going into space,' she said to her dad.

'No. I'm definitely a two-feet-on-the-ground man, myself.'

'But imagine being 200 miles from the Earth's surface and looking down on it,' said Michelle.

'You don't have to go into space to have an adventure,' said her dad.

'I know. But it's about the most exciting one you could have.'

She knew that being British and a woman would make the chances of ever being chosen to be an astronaut unlikely, but she still liked to dream about it.

'Did you want to talk about something?' her dad asked, dragging her attention away from the newspaper and the thought of going to the moon.

'I have to pick my subjects for my A-levels,' she told him.

'And you're stuck?'

Michelle nodded. 'I am. I like so many subjects and the advice I've had from school is to pick subjects I enjoy.'

Her dad laughed. 'There's plenty of time to do things you enjoy. You need to pick the subjects that are the hardest for you, because then when you master them, you'll feel incredible.'

It wasn't what Michelle thought her dad would say. She had expected a conversation where they examined each possibility in detail and arrived at the most sensible outcome. Instead, he had told her to choose subjects she found difficult. And she realised that he might be right. It was just like chess. The pleasure she felt when she won was greater when her opponent was difficult to beat. She liked things being hard.

'Do you agree?'

Michelle nodded. 'I think so. I guess that means I'm going with physics and maths, and maybe chemistry and biology because I don't know which I like best.'

Michelle started her A-levels as the British Government introduced a new scheme called 'independent learning' which was for London students studying A-levels. She didn't really understand how it would affect her until she turned up to her first chemistry lesson and instead of a teacher, the students were each given a textbook. Apparently, the government had decided that instead of being taught by teachers, the students would learn to teach themselves.

Michelle's classes were mostly science subjects. These could be dangerous as they involved experiments and labs. Nobody trusted a bunch of 17-year-old students to run a lab without some supervision, so the physics and chemistry classes were also sent a technician to be on standby. When Michelle asked where the chemistry teacher was, the technician told her that they were in the teachers' common room and were only to be interrupted if a student had a question the textbook couldn't answer.

Once the other students realised there was no teacher in attendance, most of them left, leaving Michelle pretty much alone in a classroom with the experiments to assemble. She was thrilled. It reminded her a little of building the ZX81 with her brother. She opened the first box and started to read the instructions.

Between her and the technician, the experiment was set up. While her friends sat in the sixth-form common room playing card games like spit, Michelle started teaching herself how to do **titrations**, how to create chemical reactions and how to separate **soluble** substances from **insoluble** ones.

The first time Michelle hit a topic in her textbook that she couldn't understand, she headed down to the teachers' common room and knocked tentatively on the door. The teacher came out but was clearly annoyed with being disturbed on his break, because they weren't used to students coming to the common room.

The textbook hadn't been printed in time for physics, so the headmaster had to employ a teacher called Jim Clarke to teach that class. On the first day of Michelle's physics class, she sat near the front in her favourite spot where she had an uninterrupted view of what the teacher was demonstrating to the class as well as his diagrams and explanations on the whiteboard.

After the first few classes, he started directing every question to Michelle, perhaps because she was so quiet. Embarrassed, she would often blush but managed to answer his questions. And each time she did she became more and more confident.

Soon her teacher got the class to stand up and act out physics concepts such as waves and particles by holding hands and walking around the room bouncing off the walls. By relating difficult concepts to practical examples, his way of teaching made them easier to understand and much more fun as well. Michelle began loving physics in a completely different way. She even confessed to him her dream of applying to become an astronaut and how she had clipped the advertisement from her dad's newspaper.

One day after a few months, halfway through class, Jim Clarke told Michelle to follow him to the headmaster's office. People only went there when they were in trouble, so Michelle was worried that it meant bad news. She swallowed hard and packed up her books.

Her stomach twisted in nervous knots as she followed her teacher out the door of the classroom and down the long corridor. He didn't speak so neither did she. She walked with her head down trying to think of something, anything, that she may have done that would be the reason for this. They turned down another corridor and Michelle stared down at the green carpet, realising she'd never been to this wing of the school before because the carpet colour wasn't one that she remembered.

Mr Clarke stopped outside the headmaster's office and knocked. Michelle tried to prepare for whatever trouble she was about to find herself in. He opened the door and waved Michelle through. There were a couple of tall grey filing cabinets and windows where she imagined the ex-boxer headmaster watched over his students, and a large wooden desk with piles of papers and a telephone sitting at one end. But there was no headmaster.

The room was empty.

Michelle's teacher picked up the phone receiver and said hello to someone. Then he smiled at Michelle.

'I've found you an astronaut to talk to,' he said kindly, holding out the phone to her.

Michelle's stomach spun. She wasn't in trouble at all. She was about to talk to an astronaut. A real, live astronaut.

She took the receiver and pressed it up to her ear. 'Hello,' she said in a tiny voice.

'Hello…' came the reply in a thick American accent and Michelle quickly remembered all the types of questions she had about applying to be an astronaut.

How fit do you have to be?

Can you be too tall?

What subjects should you study?

Was it worth learning a different language?

What language would that be?

Did it help if you could fly a plane?

She fired the questions into the phone and waited for the answers. As they came back down the line, she realised she didn't have a pen or paper. She'd have to store the information away in her brain.

'You have to be able to perform under stress,' said the voice.

Michelle nodded to herself. She could do that.

'You can't be too tall because you won't fit in the shuttle,' said the voice.

Michelle felt herself shrink a little. She was tall. She was taller than most of her friends, but maybe she'd stopped growing.

'Having a degree in science helps,' said the voice.

Michelle was relieved. She was on the right path.

'Have great eyesight, 20/20 vision,' said the voice.

Michelle frowned. She knew that when her brother Gary had been going blind, they had tested her to make sure she didn't have the same disease. She remembered they said her eyesight wasn't 20/20. That might be a problem.

'And you need to be really, really fit,' said the voice.

Michelle was fit. She could play outdoors for hours without getting tired.

'Thousands of people send in applications. You must work out why you should be picked above them,' said the voice.

Michelle thought through everything she'd done in her 16 years. The fact she could think logically. The fact she loved making things and pulling things apart. The fact she was happiest when being tested on the hardest problems.

Her teacher was giving her a wind-up signal, suggesting it was time to say goodbye. Michelle realised it must be costing a fortune to be phoning America.

'Thank you,' said Michelle. 'I hope you get to reach the moon one day.'

The voice laughed. 'Good luck.'

As she replaced the phone receiver, she couldn't believe she'd just spoken to someone on the other side of the world who had been inside a space shuttle. Maybe becoming an astronaut wasn't just a dream after all.

9
Off to university

Only 16 people out of 300 in Michelle's year had gone on to do their A-levels. However, this new, self-learning style had been disastrous for most of her friends, including Arvinder who was one of the smartest people she knew. In fact, it was so disastrous, that only two students passed. Michelle was one of them. She'd scored high enough to be offered a place for a double degree in physics and chemistry at Durham University in the north of England. Her parents were so happy that they took her out for a special dinner.

Durham was 275 miles (443 km) from her parents' house which meant she would be leaving home and moving into one of the university colleges on campus. While her other friends were making plans to find jobs or retake their exams at another school, Michelle packed up the few things she needed to move. Her mum had bought her a pink trunk and made her a special quilt with an astronaut on it. Michelle was thrilled about going to university and being away from home for the first time.

The train would take four hours to get to Durham, but her mum still made sandwiches for her in case she was hungry.

'I'm going to miss you so much,' said her mum, hugging her tightly. Gary had left a month or so ago for America and their mum worried the house would be too quiet without either of them at home.

'I'll be back at Christmas,' said Michelle.

Her mum hugged her even tighter. 'That's months away!'

Michelle laughed. 'Not that long.'

'You'd better go,' said her dad, as the train pulled into the station. He helped her lift her trunk into the carriage. Michelle knew her dad understood how excited she was to be leaving. He'd always appreciated her adventurous spirit.

'Bye, Dad,' she said quietly.

'You take care. Don't forget to eat sometimes,' he told her, after witnessing the hours of studying she'd do without leaving her desk, often forgetting to have meals.

'I won't.'

She left her bags in the luggage compartment and went to find a seat on the window side so she could wave to her parents as the train pulled out from Kings Cross Station.

Rather than wait, she started eating the cheese and pickle sandwiches as the train set off. Michelle had never been to Durham before, and she had no idea what to expect of university life or the town where she'd be living for the next three or so years.

All she knew was that she'd be learning about physics and chemistry. And not just from some textbooks, but from real professors.

She still hadn't decided whether she preferred physics or chemistry. She knew that to do well in chemistry she needed to improve her memory because it involved memorising formulas and chemical reactions. It was a little like learning a language, and while she loved languages, she wasn't always good at remembering lots of different formulas and chemicals. Physics was more creative and intuitive, and she felt as if that might suit her more.

She ate the last sandwich as the train sped through tiny town after tiny town, heading north.

During the first week at Durham, Michelle felt as if she'd hit the jackpot. There was so much to learn, and there were so many people who wanted to learn and were keen to have fun too. She realised that because the chemistry textbooks didn't actually arrive at the school in in time for her to use, she was far behind the other students who'd mostly attended grammar schools with teachers who had explained a lot of the background to them.

Michelle was going to have to work super hard to catch up, although when it came to working in the labs, she knew her way around better than some of the other students because she'd set up the experiments with the technician at school.

In the first week, she went to an afternoon tea with her tutor group so she could meet the other students living on campus. They each told her about the prestigious schools and colleges they'd gone too, and she realised that none of them except her had been to a comprehensive school.

Worried the university had made a huge mistake, Michelle took her concerns to her tutor who was her mentor, a sort of well-being person, to help her settle in.

She knocked on his door and waited for him to call her in. He told her to take a seat and she did, feeling nervous that she was about to expose the fact she wasn't supposed to be at Durham at all.

'How are you settling in, Michelle?'

'I love it here, but I think I should check something with you. I think the university may have made a mistake letting me in. Everybody else has been to a grammar school or a private school,' she blurted out.

'And?'

'I went to a comprehensive in London, called Eltham Green, and I don't think anyone would have heard of it,' she said.

'Oh, I see. And you think you don't belong here?'

Michelle didn't answer straightaway because she was embarrassed. She was pretty sure that university places weren't usually offered to people from comprehensive schools, and she wanted to sort it out before she settled in and began to enjoy it too much.

'I just don't want to be here if there has been a mistake,' she said finally.

Her tutor smiled, leaning back in his chair. 'Guess what…'

'What?'

'I went to a comprehensive too,' he told her. 'We do let people in from comprehensives, you know. There's nothing wrong with you.'

'Oh…' Michelle let out a surprised and somewhat relieved sigh. Her tutor, who looked a little like Barney Rubble from The Flintstones, laughed.

'I can understand it might feel like you don't belong, but I've seen your marks. Trust me, you're meant to be here.'

Thanking him, Michelle floated out of the meeting. Now that she knew being at Durham wasn't a mistake, she was going to learn everything she could and … have some fun.

*

Over the next few years, many of her classmates skipped lectures, but she went to almost all of them, asking endless questions and soaking up as much as she could. She couldn't believe how inspiring it was to actually be *taught*, and by teachers who specialised in their subjects.

By undertaking a **double degree** in physics and chemistry, she had put off making the decision about which one she preferred. Since speaking to the NASA astronaut when she was at school, she still dreamt of going into space. In her final undergraduate year at Durham, she confessed to her **Honours supervisor**, Dr Graham Russell, that she'd always wanted to be an astronaut.

Instead of laughing at her dream, Dr Russell told her he had the next best thing. He invited her to come onto his team to work on a project to grow crystals under zero gravity on the next NASA space shuttle, to test whether zero gravity would produce perfect crystals. The aim of the experiment was to see if these 'perfect' crystals could help increase the **efficiency of solar cells** made from these crystals.

Efficiency of solar cells: the amount of sunlight energy that is converted into electricity by the solar cell. It typically converts between 15% to 30% of the sun's energy that hits the cell, but as the technology develops, this percentage is gradually increasing.

Michelle was delighted. She could work on something that combined her love of science with her dream of sending things into space, in a team led by Dr Russell who, like her, loved challenging himself mentally and physically. He was a keen swimmer, and frequently swam between bays in north-east England, where the North Sea is notoriously cold and treacherous.

Between finishing her undergraduate degree and the beginning of her **PhD**, Michelle took a break and flew to America to visit her brother and uncle. She hadn't seen Gary for a couple of years, and he'd started his career in computer programming. They joked about the old ZX81 and how that had sparked his love of programming. For the first time in many years Gary had come off all the drugs he'd been on to keep his blood disease under control, and it was working. He'd defied the doctors' predictions, and now he was officially in remission. It felt very reassuring to be back kicking a football around the park as if they were kids again.

While she was in America, Dr Russell tragically drowned on his summer holidays. Michelle only learned of it when she returned to university. Everyone was shattered. Michelle had lost a good friend, her supervisor, and a project. She didn't know what to do. The NASA project to grow crystals in space had been his beloved project, and the experiment had been launched while she was away.

She decided to start looking for another university to do her PhD, even considering moving to America, when Dr Russell's wife came to her with a request. She wanted Michelle to continue her PhD at Durham in Graham's group, believing that Michelle had the skills and, with the knowledge of the team, they would mentor her through her PhD which Dr Russell would have done.

Michelle agreed.

The original plan for Michelle's PhD was to use the crystals grown in space to make more efficient solar cells, based on the assumption that they would be more perfect than the ones grown on Earth where there is gravity. However, when the shuttle returned from space, the crystals had not grown; instead there was just a giant sludgy mess.

With help from the other researchers at Durham, Michelle decided to change the direction of her thesis. She decided to combine different crystalline materials to try and capture a higher percentage of the sun's energy and produce a more efficient solar cell than was being used in solar panels at the time. As well as mastering new skills, Michelle had also developed a taste for designing her own projects and making new types of devices, that hadn't existed before.

*

When Michelle completed her PhD, her parents and her brother came to the graduation ceremony at Durham University. She couldn't stop grinning at them and could see they were bursting with pride. She loved having them close again after being away for the last few years, and she also knew that she loved physics.

With the PhD under her belt, Michelle was hungry to chase more and more difficult projects, applying for any high technology job that had the word physics in it. After interviews with many different places and lots of job offers, she ended up accepting a position at the world-famous Cavendish Laboratory at Cambridge University. And so, she headed south.

Arriving at Cambridge, Michelle was brimming with ideas, having finally found the passion that she'd decorate her bedroom in. Not that she would want to cover her carpet with laboratory equipment and results, but she was narrowing down the field she loved most. She'd discovered **quantum physics**, which studies things that are very, very small, to see what happens at atomic level. Michelle loved contemplating the world of atoms, that are *a million times smaller* than the width of a human hair. She often imagined what the world would look like if she were an atom.

Her project at the world-famous Cavendish Laboratory was to make really fast and high purity **transistors.** Billions of transistors make up the **computer chips** inside mobile phones and laptops. She had to learn ways to design and make even faster ones than were being used in these devices.

Transistors are embedded in a computer chip and act as miniature electrical switches that can turn an electronic current on or off. **Computer chip** (microchip): a set of integrated electronic circuits on a small, very thin piece of silicon – like a wafer or 'chip'.

Each time she went home to visit her parents, which wasn't as often as they'd liked, her dad would try and draw her into a game of chess, and she would find herself instead describing to him the joy she'd discovered in some new aspect of science, like the revolutionary new type of microscope that IBM had just created, which not only enabled scientists to see atoms but to move them around. They would inevitably end up in a discussion about her career, and he would always come back to the same thing he'd been saying to her since she was a little girl, 'Do the most challenging thing'.

And she was. Leaping into quantum physics, a very male-dominated field of science, was new and exciting. She had worked out that what she loved most was building something that didn't exist before. She also thought that perhaps it was an advantage that there were very few women in this area of science because she often found herself being overlooked. So she could just get on and do things. Just like when she used to play competitive chess and her opponents would sit opposite her with a gleeful expression thinking they'd win, she could once again challenge people's perceptions of what they would expect of her.

'Did you read about Helen Sharman?' her dad asked, holding up the paper.

Michelle nodded. Helen Sharman was the first Briton to journey into space.

'Not disappointed it wasn't you?'

Michelle had been thrilled when she first read the news because she always assumed that the first British astronaut would be a man. She had heard Helen Sharman speak and heard how determined she was, and it made her proud that a woman was first. She told her dad, 'I think it's great. She's a scientist too.'

Her dad laughed. 'Tell me again what you're doing?'

Michelle smiled. Explaining quantum physics in simple terms was almost impossible, and giving any detail about her research made most people's eyes glaze over unless they were also quantum physicists. 'I'm in the semiconductor physics group,' she told him.

'Not making it much clearer, I'm afraid!'

'It means I'm learning to design, **fabricate** and measure really small electronic devices to uncover fundamental aspects of how nature works.'

Her dad nodded. 'And is that a good thing?'

Michelle thought about his question. She loved her work, but she also wanted something more applicable, something where there was a tangible outcome. She'd learned an awful lot from the group she was with. 'Yes, because I've been able to figure out that what I love most is building things. But now, I really want to build something that's useful. I need a new challenge.'

It was her dad's turn to smile. 'You always do,' he said softly.

'Something where I can bring all my skills together.'

'I kept hoping you'd come back and tell me you wanted to be a grandmaster after all,' he said lightly. 'There're more women playing chess than ever.'

Michelle smiled. 'Sorry, Dad. As much as playing chess gave me that buzz for a while, it was never going to keep me engaged forever. Quantum physics gives me the same buzz, but it's there all the time. Every time I wake up, I want to get to the lab, and create something new.'

Michelle knew she was lucky to have found her 'thing'. There were plenty of people still searching.

'Tell me why this new microscope is so exciting,' her dad said.

Michelle explained exactly how the new IBM microscope changed the way humans could 'see' on the atomic scale.

'Way back around 430 BCE, the Greek philosopher, Democritus, imagined that the world was made up of tiny particles or **atoms** that couldn't be divided into anything smaller. It's only now, nearly 2,500 years later, that we've been able to see that atoms really exist. In their experiment, IBM used a very fine metal tip to trace over the surface of a crystal and 'image atoms' or see them for the very first time.'

Her dad leant back in his chair and seemed to be thinking. Michelle waited for him to finish his thought. She was used to his quiet ways.

'Sounds as if atoms are your future.'

10
Heading Down Under

As a research fellow at the famous Cavendish Laboratory in Cambridge University, Michelle was always the first one into the lab in the mornings. She liked coming in before breakfast and setting up her experiment while it was still dark outside. Not only did she like being the first in so she could work quietly in the lab on her own, but she also liked setting up her experiment early because it took hours to settle and **calibrate,** which was needed to make sure the results were accurate. While she waited, she would join one of the men's basketball matches at lunchtime on the other side of town.

> **Calibrate:**
> testing the equipment to make sure the measuring instruments were precisely accurate.

Since leaving home, Michelle had stopped playing netball, discovering instead the joys of playing basketball while she was at Durham

University. Basketball was becoming one of the more popular sports at English universities because many students were coming across from America on basketball scholarships. They struggled to find good practise games in England so had set up their own matches where anyone could turn up and play.

The first time Michelle played basketball, she loved it, even more than netball because she never had to stop running. She also loved the fact that there was always a game to be had each lunchtime. Watching the eight or so very tall men chasing down the ball and hustling to shoot reminded her of watching Gary and her dad play football when she was little. Except now she was allowed to play too, because she was tall and fast, and she could shoot.

Michelle even dreamt of playing basketball competitively and played in several county teams. She knew she wasn't that skilled at basketball compared to the Americans, but as an English player she would have a chance of going for a career in the sport. She played nearly every weekday, and it made her feel powerful and strong.

'Michelle!' one of the players yelled. He was almost seven-foot (213 cm) tall, and it wasn't hard lobbing the ball over the heads of the others to him. She threw it long and he reached up, snatching it with one hand before scoring.

The ball was already headed back down the court. Michelle chased after it, managed a steal from one of the players and dribbled on the spot as she worked out where to pass. It was a fast and furious game, like most lunchtimes, and by the time they'd played for an hour Michelle was sweaty, red-faced and puffing. As much as she delighted in scientific discoveries, she also needed to run. Perhaps she would have made the perfect astronaut candidate after all, being both physically and mentally fit. If only she'd had perfect vision.

At 28, while Michelle was at Cambridge, her mum died suddenly and unexpectedly. She was devastated and it rocked her close family, particularly as it was just a week before Gary's wedding in America. It was a turning point for Michelle. She adored her mother and without her, Michelle realised that life was finite and that more than ever it was important to spend her life doing something she felt worthwhile and passionate about.

She'd been at Cambridge for years, working as part of a large team of around 80 people, studying fundamental quantum physics in small electronic devices. She'd learned a lot in her time there. Most importantly, she had realised how much more you could get done as part of a team. She knew now that she wanted to be at the forefront of building a new technology that used quantum physics.

It was around this time in 1998, that another physicist, Bruce Kane, wrote a paper for the scientific journal *Nature*, where he suggested that it could be possible to build a quantum computer in silicon by encoding information on individual phosphorus atoms wired up with electronic circuits made of tiny transistors.

Intrigued, Michelle read his paper more than once. It was a completely new concept, which was bold and ambitious because very few people in the computing world thought of using **silicon** for quantum computing. Most scientists thought for quantum computing to work, a new type of material would have to be used.

Silicon: the most abundant element in the earth's crust, usually extracted from sand.

She took the paper into the research labs at Cambridge and spoke to some of her colleagues about it. Many disagreed with Bruce Kane, saying the precision needed to build his design of a quantum computer in silicon was beyond what was currently possible.

'But what if it's not?' asked Michelle, who hadn't been able to stop thinking about the arguments Bruce Kane had made. His idea was simple and elegant, and it was the only way she could see to build a real quantum computer that would work.

Her colleague smiled. 'Classical computers use silicon. Quantum computing won't use the same material.'

It wasn't the first time Michelle had found herself in the middle of this debate. For years since the first transistor for classical computing had been designed in 1947, engineers had integrated them onto a single chip and made them ever smaller and faster. So instead of computers needing a whole room like the ones first invented, they were now small enough to fit on a desk, like the home computer ZX81 her brother Gary had built years ago. Computer chips were all made in silicon, which was a relatively cheap material widely used for electronics and computing.

Michelle thought that silicon was also the ideal material to build a quantum computer in, but with even smaller 'quantum' transistors. These transistors would be 100-1000 times smaller than the smallest conventional transistor, all the way down to the size of atoms. She believed that making such tiny, atom-based transistors in silicon was possible. It meant adapting existing technology that was used to image atoms to both image and manipulate atoms with atomic precision.

It had never been done before, but she could see that by using the scanning tunnelling microscope, and Bruce's ideas, there was a way to make it work. But she also knew that if she stayed working in England then it wouldn't be possible. The English system was too hierarchical, and she knew she would need to work with people who were willing to try new and ambitious things. She considered going to the USA, but she also knew that researchers in the States worked in small competitive groups, and to successfully build a quantum computer, she would need to be part of a large team that collaborated with each other.

What she wanted was a university **research fellowship** somewhere that would encourage collaboration, would match her ambition and welcome it. Somewhere like Australia, she thought. She applied for an Australian Research Council Queen Elizabeth II (QEII) Fellowship to work in Sydney.

Michelle had visited Australia before when her cousins moved from England to Young in New South Wales back in the 1970s. Since then, her grandmother Hessie, had moved over in the 1980s because she was sick of the wet weather in London.

Michelle had visited her after her mum died. She remembered the gorgeous red outback landscape, the sunshine, and the beaches.

She rang Gary in America to tell him she'd been offered a fellowship in Sydney to help set up a new Centre of Excellence for Quantum Computer Technology at the University of New South Wales.

He laughed down the phone. 'I always told you that one day I'd buy you a one-way ticket to Australia. Now I don't have to!'

'Will you come and visit me?'

'Of course. It sounds perfect,' he said.

*

Her dad wondered what he had ever done to them both, with Gary living in California and Michelle now moving to Sydney. Both Gary and Michelle had always loved adventure, and while moving to Australia wasn't quite the same thing as blasting into space, it was a long, long way from London.

'Of course, I'd prefer you accepted **Stanford**,' her dad said, explaining that he missed his family and would have loved one of them to relocate near the other.

But Michelle's family were excited for her, which was more than some of her colleagues at Cambridge who looked at her strangely when she told them about her plan to move to Australia. Most of them couldn't understand why she was even considering moving Down Under. They had always believed that the standard of work being done in Europe was much higher than anywhere else in the world. Michelle was used to people thinking like that, but she didn't agree.

She tried to tell them that Australia offered something unique and different from England. Aside from the fact it didn't rain all the time, it was possible to work on large-scale, ambitious projects with academics from across the country. Despite the confused looks she had in the lab from her colleagues, Michelle knew instinctively that she'd made the right decision.

Farewelling her family and friends was hard, though. They all came to the airport to say goodbye and hugged her for what felt like hours.

Her dad understood why she was leaving. He'd always been the one to push her to challenge herself and find the thing that gave her a buzz.

'Well, Dad,' said Michelle. 'I think it's atoms I'm chasing.'

He smiled. 'Long way to go for that.'

'Come and visit when you get the chance,' she said.

'Of course. You couldn't keep us away!'

Michelle knew that she owed a lot to her parents for her success.

'One last game of chess before you go,' he said laughing as he had brought a chess board to the airport. 'It must be almost my turn to win.'

Michelle knew she had to play. It was his way of stalling a little and it was relaxing having a quick game before getting on a plane to fly to the other side of the world.

They set up the board in silence. Michelle let her dad go first. She didn't play very often now and hadn't really thought about chess since she'd discovered physics. But once she picked up her old favourite knight, she played exactly the way she always had, defensively building up her forces and only getting ready to strike when she was ready. She knew that she approached science in the same way. Never taking a risk until she could clearly see all the parts of the puzzle, making it less likely that it would be unsuccessful.

Within minutes, she saw the move her dad was planning and made her play. Five moves later, the game was done. She didn't need to say anything. Her dad lay his king on the board and reached out his hand to shake hers. It didn't seem like 20 years ago that they'd played for the first time. It seemed much more recent.

She shook his hand, his skin warm. 'You'll be fine, Mickeydoo,' he said. 'You'll be more than fine.'

Arriving in Australia in June 1999, Michelle bought her first-ever pair of sunglasses. It was winter but it was still warm and balmy, and she realised she would have to ditch her English winter wardrobe.

Within weeks of settling in Sydney, she was part of a national women-in-physics tour, flying around the country and giving lectures in different states about quantum physics.

She still hated public speaking, and from the moment she was told of the upcoming lecture series, she couldn't stop thinking about what she was going to say. She still preferred listening to others on stage rather than being in front of an audience and had to force herself to work through her fears. Sometimes she had trouble sleeping the night before a particularly busy day of talks – she realised that she'd have to find a better way to approach public speaking because it looked as if she'd be doing a lot of it in the future.

What she discovered from travelling around Australia, though, was how many amazing scientific things were happening here. Within weeks she knew she'd made the right choice moving countries and could feel her excitement growing at the potential for new possibilities in this sunburnt land.

11
Building a super tiny device

At night, Michelle dreamt of building the world's first quantum computer. She knew she wasn't the only quantum physicist with this dream, but it was something as real to her as becoming an astronaut had been when she was a teenager. She'd been living in Australia for four years and was now working on the most ambitious project she'd ever tackled. Her team at the University of New South Wales were trying to build new types of tiny transistors that would be the first step to the long road towards making a powerful quantum computer.

For a couple of months she had been working with engineers from Germany and Australia, on designing a very advanced tool called an **atomic fabricator pod**, which was a machine for building the first single-atom tiny transistors.

Working with the engineers, Michelle had come up with a plan to build the two huge stainless-steel machines in separate, adjacent rooms. In one was a **scanning tunnelling microscope** which had a fine metal tip that could be used to provide images of the atoms and could also move atoms around. The other, a **molecular beam epitaxy system**, housed a separate crystal growth system that enabled the growth of very pure silicon crystals built up one layer of atoms at a time. Nobody had ever managed to build anything like this before, because it was very difficult to get both machines to work together at the same time. And it would cost around $3.5 million.

The design project had been progressing well, but they'd hit a major problem. Michelle was on a Skype call with the engineers from Germany and some of the other key people involved in the project.

'You want lots of pumps on your crystal growth system to pump out all the air molecules and other things you don't want so that very pure crystals can grow without any defects – an ultra-high vacuum. But you also need to measure the miniscule heights of the atoms on the microscope side,' said the head engineer.

Michelle nodded. 'Yes, that's right.'

‘Well, the pumps needed to get the best vacuum cause the stainless-steel system to vibrate,’ said the engineer.

Michelle sighed. She had a feeling that she knew how this would end. It was the reason that nobody had been able to work out how to get these two systems to work at the same time. Michelle finished the engineer’s sentence, ‘And you can’t get atomic precision because the vibrations from the pumps make all the other parts of the machine shake.’

‘Correct,’ said the engineer.

Undertaking this project had been a huge risk for Michelle’s career and if she couldn’t get the system working there was no way she could move to the next part of her ambitious plan to build a quantum computer.

‘So, let’s work out our options for how to solve this,’ Michelle said.

The engineer paused for a second. Michelle was used to coming up against roadblocks. She didn’t believe for one second that they couldn’t find a way around it, just like they’d found ways around other problems.

‘I did wonder about placing the systems in different rooms,’ said the engineer.

Michelle's brain started whizzing through the idea. Within minutes she'd already jumped ahead to how they could make that work. She started nodding as the engineer went on.

'And we build acoustically sealed walls, with a tube that connects the two rooms to pass the sample from one to the other. The key thing will then be to ensure the tube is designed to stop vibrations passing from one side to the other.'

'Perfect. We just need to design the lab and the building around this new system,' said Michelle.

The engineer nodded. The energy in the room had shifted. Everyone had come to this meeting fearing the worst, but now they had a new and exciting plan. Michelle smiled. It was her first real smile in a day or so. And as she did everyone else in the room smiled too. It was possible. It was risky and difficult, but possible. Now they just had to build it.

*

One part of Michelle's job at the research centre, was meeting all sorts of people to discuss science, where future technologies were heading and what they were doing with their funding. Sometimes it was simply to meet people who had shown an interest in the ambitious projects they were focused on. One of those meetings was with Dr Thomas Barlow who was working for the Australian Government as the science advisor to the Minister for Education, Science and Training.

Michelle had met him before at a function in Canberra and invited him to visit her labs so that he could see what was happening on the project. She knew she liked him because he was friendly, intelligent, courteous and asked all the right questions.

'Tell me why quantum physics is important for computing?' he asked.

'You do know that once I start talking about this subject, we could still be here next week,' said Michelle lightly.

Thomas laughed. 'I have an hour.'

'Then I'll talk fast.'

After explaining her research in some detail, she said, 'Quantum computers will perform calculations in seconds that would otherwise take thousands of years.'

Michelle checked that Thomas hadn't fallen asleep. She knew that sometimes her passion for this subject meant people didn't quite follow what she was talking about. She had to remember that most people had no idea about quantum physics, and just the sound of some of the words made them want to run. She really wanted people to understand how exciting it was and how cutting-edge the technology could be.

She continued, 'I wake up excited every morning about my day and what is possible. Every time we achieve something in the lab it's the most amazing feeling in the world. What else could I ever do that would feel like that?'

'I start most mornings with writing,' Thomas said referring to a book on Australian innovation he was working on.

Michelle laughed and realised she had met someone who seemed to be as driven as her. 'I want to push the boundaries of what's possible.'

Thomas didn't say anything for a second and Michelle worried that she'd said too much. She was always trying to enthuse other people about how amazing quantum physics really was.

Then Thomas smiled and it was warm and genuine. 'That's brilliant,' he said.

'Thanks, Thomas,' said Michelle, feeling as if she was blushing. She wasn't used to people being so honest with her.

'Call me Tom,' he said.

Thomas, or Tom to his friends, had been at Oxford University in England for some years but was now back living in Australia, and he and Michelle talked much longer than his allocated hour. The more they talked, the more they realised how much they had in common. They both believed that Australia was a great place for science, they both played basketball and they both shared an ambition to see the potential for groundbreaking science recognised locally. When Tom gave Michelle his business card at the end of the meeting, she knew she'd see him again.

She was right. It wasn't long before the two were dating. He started joking about how he had to travel to England and then return to Australia before meeting his English rose.

The night before Michelle was to address a huge crowd, she confided in Tom how she felt about public speaking. He understood, but instead of telling her that she had to just get on with it, which other people had told her over the years, he gave her some advice.

'It's not about just surviving the public speaking; it's about learning to enjoy it. If you enjoy it, then everyone listening will too.'

'How do I enjoy it if I'm so nervous about forgetting something important that needs to be said?'

He laughed. 'Find the joy. You love talking about quantum physics more than anything else. Pretend you're boring me!'

It was her turn to laugh. 'Quantum physics is never boring!'

'It's not when *you* talk about it because you love it. So, show the audience what it means to you, and you'll start enjoying giving lectures.'

Michelle liked the idea of trying to enjoy being on a large stage because she was required to do a lot of public speaking, and the fears of her school days still loomed. She knew she had to find a strategy that would work for her.

When she next went out on stage with a microphone and looked out into the crowd of faces, she dropped her shoulders, took a large breath, and tried to relax. Then she started to talk, remembering not to make the material so complicated that nobody would understand it, but also trying to share her joy at the discoveries her team had made. By the time she reached the end of the lecture, she was surprised it had flown past so quickly. It seemed that Tom's suggestion to enjoy herself was a perfect one.

Months later, when Michelle was attending a physics conference in New Zealand, Tom went with her. They secretly decided to elope and get married in a church in the mountains of the South Island. Michelle knew that not having her mother present at a large wedding would have made her very sad, so this way the two of them would be able to enjoy the occasion just by themselves.

Later in the year, in December, her family came out from England for a big wedding celebration with all their friends and family, and with Gary and his family from the USA.

Michelle felt as if everything had slotted together. She'd found someone to share her life with who understood her ambition and drive, but who was considerably better at basketball than she was; the system they'd been building in the research lab was ready to be tested, and Australia seemed to be the perfect place for forging ahead with this pioneering technology.

*

Michelle knew the risks to her career if the system they'd spent two years building didn't work. She'd signed a waiver saying that the companies building the systems were not to blame if it didn't work. People were getting nervous about the risk, but Michelle tried not to listen to them.

There had been many times in her life when people had underestimated her abilities, and she had decided long ago that two things happened to people who were constantly told they couldn't do something. The first was that they started believing what other people were saying, and the second was that they started underestimating themselves as a result. Learning how to play and even more importantly, how to win chess had changed Michelle. She knew how often her opponents hadn't expected her to be any good, and how often she surprised them.

She knew what they were attempting was the next natural step in quantum physics and, unless a system could be built where atoms could be manipulated and then placed where they were required, she believed building a quantum computer would be impossible. She hadn't undertaken this decision lightly. She'd approached it the same way she approached chess. She'd built up her defences, she'd read the game, she'd worked out the puzzle and she knew the most likely outcome before she attacked.

It would be several days before they could see if the experiment had worked. On the third day after preparing the sample and calibrating the numerous components, everyone who had worked on the system was in the lab waiting for the outcome. Nobody was talking. The team watched silently through the glass.

Now was the moment Michelle would find out if all those years of work were worth it.

An image from the scanning tunnelling microscope was projected onto a large screen. Almost immediately they saw the shape of the atoms

on the silicon crystals pop up! Not only that, but the resolution was a factor of six times higher than they had expected.

This was the first time they had been able to see clearly atoms sticking up from the surface of their silicon crystals. Now they were able to move the atoms around and place them where they needed to be for their tiny quantum circuits.

Everyone started cheering. Michelle felt the incredible buzz she used to feel when she'd won a long, hard game of chess. She couldn't stop grinning. They'd done it. And she knew it was just the beginning.

Michelle and her team successfully build: the **atomic fabricator pod** – linking together two UHV technologies; the **scanning tunnelling microscope** – so the scientists can 'image' or 'see' individual atoms and move them to where they want to place them; and the **molecular beam epitaxy** system – to grow very pure crystals, atom layer by atom layer to finish the tiny transistors.

12
The world's smallest transistor

Michelle was up before the rest of the house. Tom and their three children, Blue, Jack and Bondi tended to sleep later than she did, so she often found herself tiptoeing around in the darkness, using the time to think about her day. She made a second cup of tea, letting it steep like her dad always would when he'd joke that it had to be so strong the spoon would stand up on its own.

Michelle had just become the Director of the Centre she'd worked in for nearly a decade, overseeing the group of 180 researchers from universities across Australia. There were several scientific teams involved, each developing different technologies to help solve the challenge of building a quantum computer.

There were many other teams of quantum physicists across the world also racing to build the world's first quantum computer, but none were using silicon the same way as Michelle. Her reason for using it was that it was one of the cleanest, purest materials on the planet and had been manufactured in large quantities for more than 50 years. And she believed the team's ability to make very accurate tiny transistors from it would eventually lead to their goal of combining tens, hundreds or even millions of transistors in a powerful new quantum computer.

Michelle thought that being the only group in the world to manufacture with atomic precision, gave them an edge on their competitors.

*

'You're still here, Mum,' said her daughter, Bondi, as she walked into the kitchen rubbing sleep from her eyes. Most days Michelle was long gone before her children left for school.

'Just planning,' said Michelle.

Bondi laughed. 'You're always planning. What are you up to now?'

Michelle knew her daughter wasn't actually asking to be told about her plans to build the world's smallest precision-built transistor in a single silicon crystal, so she said, 'Thinking about last night's game.'

'Sorry you lost,' said Bondi, helping herself to a bowl of cereal.

Michelle and Tom had played their local team's basketball final the night before and the rest of the family had cheered on from the sidelines. It hadn't helped though. They lost by three.

'Next season. What are you up to today?' Michelle asked.

Bondi shrugged. 'Maths test.'

'Are you ready for it?'

Her daughter concentrated on her bowl of muesli, dodging the question. 'Sort of.'

Michelle laughed. 'I'd better get going. I have a "sort of" day too.'

It was one of Michelle's passions to see more girls experience the joys of physics and maths, but she knew better than to start by pushing her daughter into it. Bondi would work out her own path, just like her other two children, as long as she knew that science was a possibility and not something to be avoided because she was a girl.

*

After developing the world's first devices made with the precision of the scanning tunnelling microscope, Michelle's research team were concentrating on building more precise devices at the atomic level. Many in the industry doubted that devices could ever be made where just a single atom could control its behaviour, but she pushed ahead, believing in what her lab was doing.

Sometimes it felt as if she was back at school defying the beliefs of people who doubted things until they happened. She didn't mind that feeling – seeing through complex challenges with many pathways had been part of what she'd done her whole life.

The scanning tunnelling microscope gave Michelle and her team the ability to see the single phosphorus atoms they had placed into the surface of silicon crystals and to zoom in on the beautiful quantum wave patterns formed by the electrons on the surrounding silicon atoms. For Michelle, the magic was being able to see atoms and she never tired of seeing those wave patterns.

Their most ambitious project to date was the creation of a **single-atom transistor**; something that had never been done before. To do this, Michelle's team had set out an eight-step plan. Across the world many well-known physicists doubted that the individual steps were even possible, let alone getting through all eight.

Single-atom transistor: a tiny silicon transistor where a single phosphorus atom controls the transistor operation between the digital 1 and 0 or 'on' and 'off' states.

Michelle knew that if she were working anywhere else in the world, developing this technology would have been almost impossible. It needed people with the attitude to 'give it a go'. Having moved to Australia she was sure that she could set up a unique lab full of collaborative, dedicated and adaptable scientists who were prepared to take the risk. And she believed there was a very strong chance they would be successful.

Year after year the team slogged through each of the eight steps. Now, finally, they'd reached the last step. They'd been able to see the single phosphorus atom in the centre of the device with the microscope. Now they had the agonising wait after wiring it up into an electronic circuit to see if it behaved like a transistor.

'It's working!' exclaimed Martin, one of her PhD students, as he measured the device and saw the hoped-for signature from the electrical measurements.

'No way! It's actually working!' yelled Michelle.

It was beautiful. They could see the single-atom transistor in operation. Ten years of design and planning had paid off. And it was the most incredible feeling in the world.

Later, when she was celebrating with her family, her son Blue asked her what it felt like when she saw that it had worked.

'It's the kind of feeling you have when you want to spontaneously run as fast as you can down the corridor. The kind of feeling where you have so much energy you feel like you could just take off and fly,' she told him.

He nodded. 'Yeah. Like when I've mastered a difficult piece of music on the piano.'

'Yeah,' she said. 'When you've spent years working towards something that you know has never been done before and it pays off. There really is no better feeling.'

Michelle let her family laugh and joke around her as the incredible joy of success settled in. She still couldn't quite believe they'd done it. It was years of hard work by so many students and researchers in her team and she was incredibly grateful.

*

Michelle still found explaining quantum computing and the potential of quantum physics a challenge for many audiences. Talking to secondary school students about the potential for quantum physics, Michelle told them that, 'Quantum physics is how the world behaves at its very smallest. For example, if you have a tennis ball and you throw it at a wall, in our normal world it bounces off. And you can put your hand out and catch it. But in the quantum world that ball behaves more like a wave and there's a chance that the ball won't just bounce off the wall but will go through the wall and out the other side, especially if the wall is very thin. So, it's just that when things are very small, they behave more like waves than particles.'

She showed them projections of the wave patterns that atoms make when magnified, and talked about how stunningly gorgeous she found them. She tried to explain to the students about how when IBM first made their tiny logo out of manipulating atoms, they were picking them up and placing them on a surface. But what her lab had done was to adapt the same kind of technology to silicon so that rather than just making images they were creating new types of electronic devices, quantum devices, where the behaviour was controlled by individual atoms.

This important innovation gave Michelle and her team the ability to make new types of tiny transistors, each based on a single atom in a silicon chip. When assembled in large numbers, they could apply the strange rules of quantum mechanics in a quantum computer for new ways of storing and processing information to solve problems not possible with even the most powerful existing computers.

In the long-term they were planning to use this technology to build a whole computer based on quantum principles. One that was so powerful that it would allow you to perform complex calculations in minutes that would otherwise take conventional computers thousands of years.

'Are there any questions?' Michelle asked the audience of students.

Lots of hands sprang up. Michelle pointed to one girl down in the front.

'I really like science, but I sort of have doubts about what I want to do in the future. Can you give me some advice?' the girl asked.

Michelle nodded. 'Doubt is one of the greatest strengths of being a scientist. I'm constantly doubting what I'm doing and the direction I'm going. It's important that I'm always refining what I'm doing based on the most recent data. The ability to doubt things is a hugely positive attribute. Every day you can pursue a path, but if you don't question the path and have doubts about if it's the right one then you won't seek out answers that can help guide you.

'To choose what you do in the future is a constant process. Step by step learn the skills that interest you. These will open doors so that you constantly find your own path – one that's unique to you, that's dictated by the combination of skills you choose.'

The girl smiled as if Michelle had understood something about what she was experiencing, and Michelle asked another student for their question. She moved through the audience's questions, answering them honestly, and hopefully offering the students an understanding of a field that could feel very overwhelming.

'What's your biggest achievement?'

'Building the single-atom transistor was the biggest achievement to date as it involved so many risks. We built an atom fabricator pod that had never been made before that cost $3.5 million dollars, we built a laboratory around it that cost a further $1m. We then pursued an 8-step process that had never been proven before. If any of these hadn't worked then it would have been the end of my physics career,' said Michelle.

The girl's eyes widened as if she was imagining that happening.

'At times it was scary. But deep down I was confident that the project was of high value, and that I had done all the work that could be done to make it work. I had faith in myself,' said Michelle. 'But I have to admit I'm hugely relieved that I was right!'

The girls laughed.

'Recently my lab has gone on to make the narrowest conducting wire in silicon. It's only *four atoms wide* and *one atom tall* and it has the same capability of carrying electrical current as copper metal has,' said Michelle. 'Now this might not sound that amazing, except when I tell you that this silicon wire is **50,000 times thinner than the width of a human hair**!'

Michelle knew that this would be hard for them to imagine. Without having the ability to see the technology directly she knew it would be difficult to understand that they were making devices so small that there was no way you could see them with the human eye. It still amazed her that the technology they had developed would be responsible for building something so small yet invaluable and vital for the development of future atomic-scale electronic circuits.

'I won't go into the physics of these wires too much except to say that the reason this is such an exciting development is that the smaller we can make components like transistors and conducting wires, the smaller and more powerful we can make computer chip components.'

She'd reached the end of her hour talk to the students and made her way off the stage. The school wasn't that different from the comprehensive she'd attended back in London, and she knew that the fact that she'd had such an involved and engaged physics teacher when she was doing her A-Levels helped bring the subject alive for her. She hoped that her talks would do the same for the next generation of young scientists, but she knew an even better way would be to open her laboratories each year for primary and secondary students to come and see the technology directly.

From that day on, each year she decided to hold a school open day. Quantum physics was a male-dominated field, but she truly believed that she saw the world in a different way from her male colleagues and that having more people with different ways of thinking in the field could only be a good thing. By opening the doors to her laboratories, young people would get to see a distinct world of possibilities.

13
Back to school

Michelle had just returned to her hotel in France with Tom after a ceremony where she was awarded the international *L'Oréal-UNESCO For Women in Science Award* in recognition of her pioneering research in quantum physics. Tired but thrilled at the award, Michelle flopped down onto their large hotel bed and kicked off her shoes.

She'd never dreamed that one day she'd be winning awards worth over $100,000 in prize money, or that a camera crew would be arranging to take her back to her old school and film her walking through the playground, while she took them on a tour of her teenage years.

It was funny thinking about her childhood in England, how she really didn't feel very different now from who she was when she sat down opposite her dad to play chess. She was still just as determined. She was still just as passionate about how she approached life, only now her work involved atomic level precision of atoms and not chess pieces.

Her phone beeped with messages from Blue, Jack and Bondi wanting photos and details about what she'd eaten at the special ceremony. It was late because of the time difference but she sent them a photo of Tom in front of a view of the Eiffel Tower from their hotel room.

She'd won other awards over the past ten years, but there was something about this one that was special. It was the first-ever award that had been established to celebrate women in science. She always felt awkward winning awards, but they had an effect that she found was important because they encouraged other women to enter the field. They also made it easier to attract funding for the research lab, which meant they could continue pushing the technology and progressing their commitment to building a quantum computer.

She went to sleep dreaming of space as she used to when she was little, wondering if at the age of 50 she could still become an astronaut.

*

It had been a long time since she'd been back to Eltham Green. As she walked towards the bottom gate with the camera crew trailing after her and filming, she thought how strange it was that she was returning to the place that had been so instrumental in her science education. It was here that she had learned to teach herself and it was here that she had met her wonderful physics teacher, Jim Clarke. Perhaps there was something in that, she thought, that chasing the answers to science when she was a teenager had made her more determined in her career. And having a teacher passionate about the subject certainly inspired her.

Michelle looked up at the roof, half expecting to see their old headmaster standing with his binoculars trained on the playground below, waiting for a fight to break out. She knew he'd retired and that it was a different headmaster now, but she liked imagining Mr Dawson was still patrolling the place.

She told the camera crew about him and one of them laughed. He knew all about the rumours surrounding the school because he'd seen the movie *Clockwise* based on the school, where British actor John Cleese had played the role of the headmaster.

'It's amazing how little this place has changed,' said Michelle.

'Let's start rolling then,' said the camera operator as the students started streaming through the bottom gate.

She wished Gary was with her because they could have had a bit of a laugh about all the things that happened while they were at the school. As the children came through the gate and saw the camera crew, they became excited.

'What's going on?' one of them shouted. Students crowded around and were jumping up and down to get into the line of the camera. They had never seen a camera crew at school before and were intensely interested and excited to see what was happening.

Michelle found this rather funny, particularly as this was the exact spot where she had experienced her first 'fight' with Stacey.

Before long she found herself slipping into the south-east London accent and mucking around with them, trying to explain that she used to go to the school many years ago.

'Who here loves physics?' she shouted into the crowd. Sensing that they would all get on TV if they answered in the right way, they shouted 'me!', and 'me!' and 'me!'. This wasn't the type of reaction Michelle typically got when asking that question, so she decided to continue, 'Who here knows Marie Curie?'

Again, the reaction was funny as they started shouting out 'Me!'.

Michelle found herself telling them that she went to the school back in the 1980s and loved physics. She told them that she was now a Professor of Physics in Sydney and was coming back to the school as she had recently won a science award from the French company, L'Oréal.

'What, the makeup company? Are you serious?' exclaimed one kid.

Michelle started laughing. How bizarre it must all seem to them, a camera crew with a French accent filming this woman who had come from Australia to accept an award for physics, and ended up visiting her old school in Eltham. It was even funnier because Michelle was allergic to makeup, so never wore any.

*

While she was in London, she also visited her father for a few days, even challenging her dad to a game of chess. He had retired, but she could tell that he was still as sharp as a button and delighted to have a game.

'I still don't really understand what it is you're doing,' he said. 'But I pretend to know and nobody else understands either, so I can say all sorts of things.'

Michelle laughed. 'It's true. Explaining quantum physics is hard because it's highly mathematical and very visual. I think, it's going to be part of my life's work to be able to get people to understand the significance of quantum physics and quantum computing.'

Even though they hadn't played in years, as soon as they sat down, they both assumed their serious 'chess face' poses. They found it easy to slot back in, eyeballing each other every now and then with a look that signalled how happy they were to be there.

'Do you remember Gary's old computer?' Michelle asked.

'Yes! Remember, he'd always yell out to be careful when you came into his room – not to shut the door too roughly because it was so fragile, it would stop working,' said her dad.

They laughed at how the computer in all its clunky glory was once the envy of every school kid at Eltham Green. Now it was like one of those large, old-fashioned analogue radios. And one day Michelle hoped, the laptop she used at home, would be the same. Outdated, slow and a museum piece because she would have been part of the next computing revolution, the quantum computing revolution, which would see computers get smaller, faster, and super powerful.

14
Australian of the Year

Michelle had been in Australia for 19 years when she was announced as a nominee for Australian of the Year in 2018. She didn't know who had nominated her and didn't really know what it entailed. In her mind, she was still the shy introvert who avoided public speaking all through her school years and had dodged questions about her private life ever since becoming a leader in quantum physics.

Now she was heading to the airport to fly to Canberra for the ceremony with Tom and their kids.

'Mum, you've checked you have your speech, three times,' said Bondi.

'I know. But I don't want to forget to bring it!'

'Will we get to meet the Prime Minister?' Blue asked.

'Maybe,' said Michelle.

'And eat really yummy food?' asked Bondi.

Michelle laughed. 'I don't know. I've never been to this event before, but I'm sure there will be something to eat.'

'Hope you win, Mum,' said Jack.

'I don't think I will. I'm pretty sure they would have given me a heads up if I had, and there are some amazing nominees.'

'You're a champion to me, regardless,' said Tom with a smile.

Michelle had read all about the other nominees from the other states and territories. They were a very impressive bunch, including JT, the NRL player from Queensland, the actor Samuel Johnson and the craniofacial surgeon, Professor David David (yes, that's his real name!). The idea that a girl from a rough comprehensive school in London's inner southeast, would one day find herself on the other side of the world in a fancy outfit waiting to hear if they were Australian of the Year was so far-fetched that Michelle felt as if she was living in an alternate universe.

On the plane, she stared out the window and watched the landscape change beneath her. She had loved flying ever since she was a child and had even taken flying lessons. She always stole the window seat so that Tom, with his long legs, could sit in the aisle.

She knew she should be reading over her speech to make sure it was okay, but she really didn't think there was much point. She was pretty sure JT would win because he was such an Australian icon. It was a lovely honour just to be nominated.

*

A couple of hours later, Michelle was sitting in the Great Hall of Parliament House in Canberra with a thousand guests and butterflies in her stomach, waiting to hear the winners. Tom was sitting next to her, holding her hand. She kept squeezing his fingers so tightly that he'd wiggle them a bit so that she would let go.

'Sorry,' she whispered, knowing she was crushing his hand.

He smiled at her in the dark. 'Breathe,' he mouthed.

She tried to take a deep breath as the Prime Minister, Malcolm Turnbull, began making his speech.

'We're gathered here tonight in the Great Hall of the Australian Parliament on the land of the Ngunnawal people, and we pay our respects to their elders past, present and emerging...'

The Great Hall was still and quiet. Everyone listened as the winners were announced in the other categories. High school mathematics teacher, Eddie Woo from Sydney was the Local Hero; Women's Football champion, Samantha Kerr from Western Australia was the Young Australian of the Year; and ANU biophysicist Dr Graham Farquhar was the Senior Australian of the Year.

'It's a good night for science,' said Tom quietly.

She rolled her eyes at him. He'd been teasing her for days that she was going to win. As Prime Minister Turnbull reached the Australian of the

Year category, Michelle fidgeted in her seat. She wondered how the other nominees were feeling and if they were as ridiculously nervous as she was.

Then she heard the words, 'launching Australia into the space race of the computing era,' and her eyes widened in amazement as she realised it was her.

The Prime Minister spoke into the microphone. 'And the 2018 Australian of the Year is Professor Michelle Yvonne Simmons.'

Michelle couldn't move. She felt glued to her chair. The crowd started applauding and Tom lent across and whispered in her ear.

'I think you'd better stand up.'

She squeezed his hand as she got to her feet. She turned to the children who were all staring open-mouthed in shock, as was she. She saw them all start to smile and suddenly realised the TV cameras were on her … and them! Then she saw Ian Jacobs, her Vice Chancellor, who was beaming from ear to ear.

None of them could believe it. She started to make her way through the crowd towards the stairs at the side of the stage. Her heart was beating faster than it did when she played basketball hard, she felt as if she was floating.

On the stage, the Prime Minister shook her hand and then walked her to the microphone before leaving her alone in front of a very large crowd. She knew her family overseas wouldn't be watching because they didn't really understand what it meant, but Tom's family were watching, and they would be rather surprised.

She looked up and into the lights.

'Wow…' she said, feeling quite overwhelmed. There were a few laughs from the crowd. Then she looked down at her speech and started reading.

'This is an amazing moment. I came to Australia because I believed it would allow me to realise my dreams…'

Michelle paused for a second as the news of what had just happened started to settle in. It was the same sort of buzz she'd felt when she won the London chess championship all those years ago, but this time so much more exhilarating.

Michelle went on with her speech, 'I pinch myself every day because what we are doing at the University of New South Wales in Sydney is extraordinary. We're pushing the forefront of technology to manipulate individual atoms and create new devices that have never existed before.

Atoms are totally unforgiving, and my team take on incredibly hard scientific challenges. They're people with huge dedication and grit – and they need it!

'Ultimately, we've set ourselves an audacious goal here in Australia to build not just a quantum computer, but a quantum computing industry. We're up against the likes of Google, IBM and Microsoft, and if I lived in any other country, I'd be worried. But we've proven time and again that Australian researchers have some unique advantages.

We collaborate across boundaries, but we also compete hard. We're down-to-earth, judge by results and believe in what is real. Our distaste for authority means we think for ourselves. Best of all, we're prepared to give difficult challenges a go.

'I firmly believe there is no better place on earth to be a scientist and to challenge what's possible. And as someone who was not born in this country, it's a huge honour – and a great surprise – to be recognised today … But I'm not just a scientist. As a physicist, I'm also a woman in a man's world and I'd like to say just a few words about that.

‘Throughout my career, I have found that people often underestimate female scientists. In some ways, this has been great for me as it has allowed me to work under the radar and get on with things! But I am also conscious that, when a person starts to believe what others think of them, it is easy for belief to evolve into a self-fulfilling prophecy. This is one reason I’ve always felt it’s important not to be defined by other people’s expectations of who you are or what you might be.

‘I believe women think differently and that diversity of thought is invaluable to research and technological development. I am not a fan of mandating equal numbers of men and women in all careers. However, I am a fan of ensuring that young people – all young people, male and female – pursue what they love, set their sights high, tackle the hardest tasks in life, and be the creators, rather than just the users, of technology. Some of this can be instilled at school and at university, but much of it has got to come from within. This is true for anyone – but especially for women.

‘In the same way that we must defy the expectations of others, it is important also to defy the expectations we place on ourselves. In my life

I've really lived to four mantras: do what's hard, place high expectations on yourself, take risks and do something that matters.

'But I've also come to realise I'm very fortunate to live in a country that not only accepts these ideals but celebrates them. And that says something very important about Australian society. That is why I say to all those young people out there who have got dreams that they are following: be proud of your country and of who you are. Know that reward comes from hard work, and that some of the biggest rewards come from taking on the biggest challenges. And understand that there are as many opportunities here as there are anywhere else in the world.

'Unlike me you don't have to go overseas to realise your dreams. You can realise them right here. Just look into your own heart and look to your own land.'

*

Michelle knew as she finished her speech, that for her, she had taken the hardest road she could. She had moved countries, taken massive risks in her career, pursued some of the hardest concepts in quantum physics and chased the dream she'd had for a very long time – to one day build a quantum computer that could do in seconds what would take a classical computer thousands of years. She might have a long way to go still, but just like that first game of chess, she truly believed it was possible. And on Monday morning when she was back in the lab with her research team around her, they would celebrate this recognition collectively and continue their journey together.

Glossary

- **An atom:** a tiny particle that has a nucleus (centre) of protons and neutrons surrounded by a cloud of electrons. Different elements (eg. gold, oxygen, iron, etc.) have different numbers of protons in their atoms – that's what makes them different from each other.
- **Double degree:** a university qualification usually completed in less time than two single degrees. Most undergraduate degrees (or bachelor's degree) take three years, a double degree usually takes four. It means you are studying two degrees at once and can specialise in two subject areas.
- **Fabricate:** to make or manufacture something.
- **Honours supervisor:** an academic (teacher at university) who guides the student through their Honours year research project – offering advice, encouragement. Honours is another year of mainly research after completing an undergraduate degree, and the qualification is written: BSc(Hons) if it's a Bachelor of Science Honours degree.
- **PhD:** abbreviation for Doctor of Philosophy (although you can have a PhD in any area of research, not just philosophy). A research degree is the highest level of academic qualification. It takes 3-4 years of full-time work. Students write a thesis which can be up to 100,000 words.

- **Phosphorus:** an element found in the earth's crust in very small quantities – about 1 gram per kilogram. Michelle uses the electron and nuclear spin of the phosphorus atom as the quantum bit or 'qubit'.
- **Research fellowship:** position at a university where an experienced researcher is employed to do research only (no teaching). They often work in teams of other researchers investigating a problem, some of whom might be undertaking a PhD in the area.
- **Stanford:** Stanford University is a famous research university in California, USA.
- **Soluble/Insoluble:** soluble substances dissolve in water (like sugar and salt) whereas insoluble materials (like plastic or metals, such as gold) do not.
- **Titration:** the method used to work out the concentration of a substance in a solution.
- **Ultra-high vacuum (UHV):** a vacuum regime of very low pressures, such as that found in outer space, where there is very little air and hardly any water. UHV conditions are created by pumping the gas out of a stainless-steel chamber to create a very clean environment in which to grow very pure crystals.

About the author

Nova Weetman has published 16 books for children and young adults, including: *The Secrets We Keep*, *The Secrets We Share*, *Sick Bay*, *Elsewhere Girls* and *The Edge of Thirteen*. Her latest book is *The Jammer*. Nova's books have been CBCA Notables, shortlisted for the Readings Children's Prize, Japan's Sakura Medal, the NSW Premier's History Prize and more. She won the ABIA Award for Best Children's Book Small Publisher in 2021 for *The Edge of Thirteen*. Before writing books, she worked in television. Nova is a regular on ABC Radio Melbourne talking about historic children's books in Australia.